The Hermitage
Picture Gallery

ALFA-COLOUR ART PUBLISHERS
St Petersburg
1999

The Main (Jordan) Staircase

Foreword by *Mikhail Piotrovsky*
Selection by *Sophia Kudriavtseva*
Essays and notes on the plates
by *Sophia Kudriavtseva*
(Italian, Spanish, English and French Painting)
and *Alla Kamchatova* (Netherlandish, Flemish
and Dutch, German, and Russian Painting)
Translated from the Russian by *Paul Williams* (essays)
and *Valery Fateyev* (notes on the plates)
Designed by *Vasily Bertels*
Computer layout by *Nina Sokolova*
Photographs by *Darya Bobrova*, *Pavel Demidov*,
Leonid Kheifets, *Yury Molodkovets*,
Victor Savik, *Vladimir Terebenin* and *Oleg Trubsky*
Colour correction of the transparencies
by *Vladimir Krakovsky* and *Peter Krakovsky*
Managing editor *Nina Grishina*

The colour-separated films produced by the Goland Company
PRINTED IN FINLAND

The Hermitage is one of the largest museums in the world with stocks approaching three million works of art and other items. It has a number of different departments that reflect the breadth and depth of its collections. Undoubtedly, however, it is best known among the general public worldwide for its picture gallery. Indeed the history of the museum is reckoned to have begun with the acquisition by Catherine the Great in 1764 of 225 paintings by Western European artists. The Empress's passion for collecting soon led her into other areas, notably gemstones, but paintings remained her first love.

The story of how the Hermitage picture gallery grew is a fascinating one. In the eighteenth and early nineteenth centuries, as well as single works bought and commissioned, whole collections were purchased causing a sensation among contemporaries. Among others Catherine acquired the celebrated collections assembled by the Saxon minister Count Brühl, Baron Pierre Crozat, and Sir Robert Walpole. Her grandson, Alexander I, followed her lead by purchasing the Malmaison collection, formerly the property of Napoleon's first wife Josephine Beauharnais, the collection of the Spanish minister Manuel de Godoy, and that of the Amsterdam banker Coesevelt. Later individual acquisitions became the rule until 1917, after which whole collections, newly nationalised, again came into the museum. There have been some interesting occurrences over the years — two halves of a picture reunited in the Hermitage after being separated many decades before; an Old Master "discovered" unexpectedly at an exhibition in the Russian capital; a canvas captured on the high seas by pirates; radical changes of attribution and interpretation.

The story is not only one of acquisition, however. There have been two darker periods in the history of the Hermitage picture gallery. The first came in the middle of the nineteenth century when Tsar Nicholas I decided on his own initiative that a large group of works were unworthy of the collection and put them up for sale, with the resultant loss of several important paintings. The second followed the establishment of Soviet power when a number of masterpieces were sold to foreign collectors in an attempt to fill the empty coffers of the state.

The Hermitage picture gallery today covers virtually the whole scope of Western European art from the Early Renaissance up to the beginning of the twentieth century. The Italian collection contains masterpieces by Leonardo da Vinci, Raphael, Giorgione and Titian, Tintoretto, Veronese and Caravaggio.

View of the Hermitage from the Palace Bridge

The tremendous contribution of the Low Countries is reflected in a collection that includes Rubens, Van Dyck and a whole room of Rembrandts, as well as the intriguing works of the "Small Dutch Masters". The Spanish collection, although far less comprehensive, can still boast works by El Greco, Murillo, Velazquez, Ribera and Zurbaran, and, a relatively recent acquisition, a female portrait by Goya. The stocks of English paintings are, likewise, not particularly large, but they do contain one of Gainsborough's best works and two paintings commissioned from Reynolds by Catherine the Great. Germany is represented by a collection that begins with Cranach and includes some splendid works by the Romantic artist Caspar David Friedrich. The French collection is replete with masterpieces reflecting that country's long artistic tradition from seventeenth-century Classicism to the French Impressionists and beyond them to Picasso and Matisse.

All these fine works of painting are housed in a superb setting that helps to make the Hermitage unique among the world's greatest repositories of art.

The museum was part of the imperial residence and the palatial grandeur of its interiors reflects that fact. Adjoining the mid-eighteenth-century Winter Palace is a complex of three main buildings constructed over almost a century: the Small Hermitage built by Vallin de la Mothe and Velten in the 1760s and 1770s, the Old Hermitage added by Velten in the 17s70s, and the New Hermitage, purpose-built between 1838 and 1852 to the design of Leo von Klenze in order to house the growing museum collection.

The Hermitage is famous for its ability to survive. It has endured successive evacuations in the course of three wars, the great Winter Palace fire of 1837, and the storming of the palace in 1917. The Hermitage weathered the period of revolutionary catastrophes, survived despite selling sprees and wholesale redistribution of stocks between museums. It escaped the clutches of Nazi plunderers and continued to be the chief cultural "window on Europe" for Soviet Russia.

The Hermitage has always been a museum that looks outwards to the world. To a significant extent it can be said to have been one of the main expressions of the policy of openness towards Europe initiated by Peter the Great. After becoming a public museum, the Hermitage played an immense educational role, giving those active in Russian culture access to the wider world; and later introducing the ordinary people of Socialist Russia to the fundamentals of world art.

Today the Hermitage is again actively filling its storerooms and its displays. The museum is constantly expanding, seeking to put everything it has on show. Work is currently underway to implement a major plan for the general reconstruction of the Hermitage. The Menshikov Palace has been restored to become a new centre of museum life. The Hermitage Theatre has been reconstructed and theatrical activities have become an important element in the Hermitage's existence. The Winter Palace of Peter the Great, discovered during excavations and now restored, has been opened to the public. Restoration of the stateroom interiors and reconstruction of the main exhibitions is continuing. Construction of a special repository, where the famous "reserves" of the Hermitage will be made accessible to researchers and ordinary visitors alike, is drawing to a close. Work is going on to create a fundamentally new Museum of Decorative Art in the General Staff building. The Hermitage has many plans and much work to do.

MIKHAIL PIOTROVSKY

Director of the Hermitage
Professor of Historical Sciences
Corresponding Member
of the Russian Academy of Sciences
and the Russian Academy of Arts

Italian
Painting *14th to 20th Century*

T he world-famous Hermitage picture gallery opens with the Italian school. Even the most complete collection, however, could not contain all the superb works created in the beautiful homeland of European art. For almost five centuries, Italy was the leading artistic centre in Europe, only giving way to France in the nineteenth century. The Hermitage collection reflects this long dominance. It began to come together under Peter the Great, but the most significant acquisitions were made in the time of Catherine the Great, when that Empress actively bought up noted private collections. In 1769 her agents paid the large sum of 5,000 roubles for *The Holy Family* by Cesare de Sesto, believing it to be a genuine Leonardo. A milestone in the history of the Hermitage was the acquisition in Paris in 1772 of the extremely rich collection of Pierre Crozat, Baron de Thiers. It included such masterpieces as Raphael's *Holy Family*, Giorgione's *Judith* and Titian's *Danaë* and laid the basis for the Italian collection.

In 1799 the Hermitage acquired the famous collection of the British prime-minister Sir Robert Walpole, substantially expanding its stock of Italian Renaissance and seventeenth-century works. In 1814 Alexander I bought Empress Josephine's Malmaison collection which included some superb examples of Italian art, in particular a work by the well-known sixteenth-century master Andrea del Sarto. Until the mid-nineteenth century, Italian pictures were mainly acquired outside of Italy — in England, Holland, and France. In 1850 masterpieces by Titian and Veronese came from the centuries-old collection of the Venetian Barbarigo family. All the Titians in the Hermitage, with the exception of *Danaë* and *Portrait of a Woman*, come from this source.

The Italian department owes much to Stepan Gedeonov, director of the museum in the 1860s and 1870s. It was Gedeonov who in 1865 arranged the acquisition of Leonardo's *Madonna and Child*, then in the collection of Duke Litta in Milan. In 1871 he acquired Raphael's *Madonna with a Book*, the pride of Count Conestabile's collection in Perugia. The sale of the painting to Russia was seen as a national tragedy and the owner was obliged to publish a brochure explaining his decision.

At the end of the nineteenth century the Hermitage's financial position worsened, inevitably slowing the growth of the collection. The last valuable acquisitions for the Italian department before 1917 were the *Madonna* from a diptych of the *Annunciation* by Simone Martini and a reliquary bearing a depiction of Christ with angels painted by Fra Angelico that was bequeathed by Count Grigory Stroganov in 1911. The most important event in the early-twentieth-century history of the Hermitage was the arrival of a second Leonardo — the *Madonna with a Flower* from the collection of the St Petersburg architect Leonty Benois. The work had been in the Benois family since the 1820s and was considered to be by an unknown artist of Leonardo's circle. The first scholar to suggest it was by the great artist himself was the curator of the Hermitage picture gallery Ernest von Liphart.

The appearance at that late date of a "new", unknown Leonardo caused a real sensation and quite some time had to pass before authoritative scholars from various countries approved the attribution and it assumed its rightful place in the narrow circle (perhaps a dozen) of his authenticated works that have come down to us today. The painting was valued at 500,000 francs, the best museums in the world sought to purchase it, but Benois's widow preferred it to remain in Russia and sold it to the Hermitage for much less.

After the 1917 revolution many works of Italian painting came into the Hermitage from the nationalized collections of the Stroganov, Sheremetev, Yusupov and Shuvalov families. It was from the collection of Count Pavel Stroganov, one of the first in Russia to acquire paintings by Proto- and Early Renaissance artists, that the main works from those periods came into the Hermitage. Sadly such paintings had evoked little interest among collectors when the imperial painting collection was in its glittering heyday.

In the nineteenth century painting in Italy was overshadowed by sculpture and the magical art of opera. The names of Italian painters of this period were almost unknown to European collectors. Interest in Italian fine art began to revive in the early twentieth century with the appearance of the first avant-garde tendencies — Futurism and metaphysical painting. The Hermitage's small collection of Italian twentieth-century painting formed to a large extent by chance, from collections nationalized after 1917, acquisitions from exhibitions, gifts, and even exchanges in the 1920s between Italian and Russian artists.

The 1920s also saw the start of unprecedented sales of the Hermitage's finest paintings abroad. The Italian collection was among those especially affected. The Soviet state badly needed money to restore an economy destroyed by war and revolution. The sales began gradually, cloaked in strictest secrecy. At first works by second-rate artists and objects of applied art went to auctions and private Western collections, but the money thus obtained proved inadequate. So, in the early 1930s, major Western collectors who did business with Soviet Russia — G. Gulbenkian, head of *Iraq Petroleum*, the American millionaires Armand Hammer and Andrew Mellon (U.S. Treasury Secretary) — compiled a shopping-list of Italian, Flemish, Dutch, Spanish and French paintings in the Hermitage. The Mellon collection, for example, acquired some priceless treasures: two masterpieces by Raphael, the *Madonna Alba* and *St George*, Boticelli's *Adoration of the Magi*,  Titian's *Venus before the Mirror*, and works by Veronese and Perugino. The sad list of magnificent works lost during this period could be continued. Now the former Hermitage treasures adorn American museums and private collections around the world as testimony to a dark and shameful page in this country's history.

The earliest Italian paintings in the Hermitage date from the thirteenth and fourteenth centuries, the Proto-Renaissance period. At that time the mediaeval Gothic and Byzantine traditions were still very strong. The Stroganov collection provided a cross bearing a depiction of the crucified Christ signed by Ugolino di Tedice who lived in Pisa in the second half of the thirteenth century. An indubitable masterpiece is the *Madonna* by the great fourteenth-century Sienese master Simone Martini that was once the left-hand panel of a diptych. (The right-hand panel depicting the Archangel Gabriel is in the National Gallery in Washington.)

Two works — the painting on the wooden reliquary and a fresco (a rarity in museum collections) depicting the Madonna and Child, St Dominic and St Thomas Aquinas that once adorned the walls of a monastery in Fiesole — belong to one of the greatest artists of the fifteenth century, Fra Angelico.

The fifteenth century is also represented in the Hermitage by superb works of great artists, such as Filippo Lippi, Perugino and Boticelli, but the pride of the collection is undoubtedly the paintings of the giants of the High Renaissance. The Hermitage can boast the two Leonardos already mentioned, as many Raphaels and Giorgiones, and eight canvases by Titian. Further testimony to the glory of the Venetian school, of which Titian was the acknowledged head, comes in the shape of works by the finest figures of the late sixteenth century — Tintoretto, Veronese and Jacopo Palma the Younger.

The Hermitage collection of seventeenth-century Italian art is one of the most significant in Europe. There are superb examples of the work of the founders of the Bolognese school, two Caracci brothers, Guido Reni, Domenico and Guercino. Among the masterpieces is a single work by Caravaggio, the creator of a powerful realistic tendency, one of the precursors of the Baroque style. The influence of his painting on contemporaries can only be compared with that of the Renaissance giants in their day. Caravaggio had devoted followers in other countries — France, Spain, Holland and Flanders.

In the eighteenth century only the Venetian school continued to uphold the fame of Italian painting. The Hermitage has works by the great master of monumental frescoes and superb painter Tiepolo and the landscape artists Canaletto and Guardi. The collection is worthily closed by two still lifes from the talented twentieth-century artist Giorgio Morandi, convincing proof of the undying traditions of the great Italian school.

Works by Simone Martini, the leading artist of the Sienese school, can be extremely rarely found in museum collections. This Hermitage masterpiece is the right-hand panel of The Annunciation diptych. The left wing with a representation of the Archangel Gabriel is at the National Gallery in Washington. Martini interpreted the religious scene with an exquisite and even secular grace.

NICCOLO DI PIETRO GERINI
(MENTIONED BETWEEN 1368 AND 1415)
The Crucifixion with St Mary and St John

The Crucifixion *painted in the second half of the four-teenth century by the Florentine artist Niccolo di Pietro Gerini was mentioned in the manuscript catalogue of the Count Pavel S. Stroganov collection, whence it came to the Hermitage, as a work by one of Giotto's followers. The traditions of mediaeval painting are still well pronounced in the conventional treatment of the figures represented on a flat gilded background and in a symmetry and balance of the composition. The four capital Latin letters,* I.N.R.I, *above the cross are the initials for* Jesus Nazarenus Rex Iudeorum, *that is, Jesus of Nazareth, King of the Jews. This inscription placed on the cross meant to explain why Jesus was crucified. At the foot of the crucifix, on a knoll symbolizing Calvary, is depicted the skull of Biblical Adam who, as legend has it, was buried under Golgotha. The gilded Gothic frame is inscribed:* PATER.NOSTER.QVIES.INCELIS.SANTIFI *[Our father, living in the Heavens].*

FRA BEATO ANGELICO DA FIESOLE
(CA. 1400–1455)
The Virgin and Child with Angels
Ca. 1425

Fra Beato Angelico, *one of the most poetic and elevated artists of the Early Renaissance, took monastic vows and spent the entire life in hard work painting frescoes in monasteries near Florence. His representations of saints are pervaded with a serene religious feeling. The colour range of* The Virgin and Child with Angels *looks like a festive chord built up of the Virgin's red and blue clothes and the soft radiance of the Angels' wings against the brilliant gold of the background. The vessel with lilies under the Madonna's throne symbolizes the purity of the Virgin Mary.*

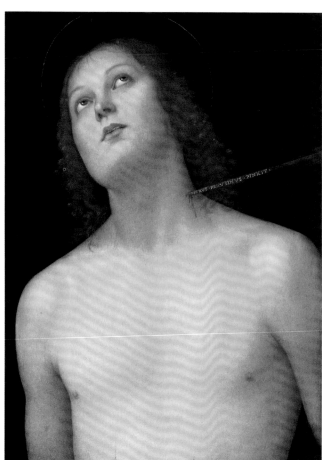

PIETRO PERUGINO (CA. 1450–1523)
St Sebastian
Ca. 1495

Pietro Perugino is a well-known master
of the Early Renaissance, a representative
of the Umbrian school of painting, Raphael's
pupil. The tragic and beautiful image of
the saint painted by Perugino is imbued with
an almost elegiac sorrow, quiet and neglect
of earthly things. On the arrow which pierced
the saint's neck, the artist put his signature
in gold: Petrus Perusinus pinxit [Painted
by Pietro Perugino].

FILIPINIO LIPPI (1457–1504)
The Adoration of the Infant Christ
Mid-1480s

The father of Filippino Lippi, Fra Filippo,
a well-known Florentine painter, was a monk
in his youth, but he ran away from the monastery
with a young nun who became his wife.
This romantic union brought forth the author
of The Adoration of the Infant Christ, whose
art is marked by noble elegance and refinement.
The poetic and sublime art of Filippino Lippi
was formed under the influence of the great
Quattrocento master Sandro Botticcelli.
The artist depicted the Virgin and the Child
Christ amidst fragile, nearly fleshless angels
in Paradise, which is designated as a small
terrace separated by a balustrade from a lifelike
yet perfectly harmonious landscape.

GIORGIONE
(GIORGIO DA CASTELFRANCO)
(1478?–1510)
Judith

The first great Venetian painter marking the age of the High Renaissance, Giorgione lived a short life — the celebrated master was about thirty-two when he became a victim of smallpox. Only about a dozen of authentic works by Giorgione have reached us. Judith *is one of the Hermitage's masterpieces. In the Crozat collection the canvas was ascribed to Raphael. In 1968 the Hermitage restorers carried out a very complex work of recreating the original appearance of the painting spoiled by subsequent over-paintings and the layers of old, darkened varnish, saturated with grease. After several years of work* Judith *has acquired its former appearance shining with a wealth of its light and pure colours.*

LEONARDO DA VINCI
(1452–1519)
*The Madonna with
a Flower
(The Benois Madonna)*
1478

T*he history of how this
masterpiece by Leonardo
came to St Petersburg is very
interesting. The picture was
the property of the Astrakhan
merchant Sapozhnikov,
whose daughter married
the St Petersburg architect
Leonty Benois. Sapozhnikov
told that he had acquired this
painting at Astrakhan from
a strolling Italian musician.
Later this beautiful legend
was refuted, but it still remains
unknown when and how this
unique work from the great
artist's early period, arrived
in Russia. The work is an oil
painting, which was a new
medium in that period.*

LEONARDO DA VINCI (1452–1519)
*The Madonna and Child Christ
(The Litta Madonna)
Ca.* 1490

In 1482 Leonardo was employed by Lodovico Moro, the Duke of Milan. At his court he painted, in the technique of tempera traditional for Italy, The Madonna and Child Christ, *generally known as* The Litta Madonna *after her Italian owner, the Milanese Count Antonio Litta. The image of the Madonna embodies an ideal of beauty.*

RAPHAEL (RAFAELLO SANTI) (1483–1520)
The Holy Family (The Madonna with the Beardless St Joseph)
Ca. 1506

In 1504 Raphael, already one of the most famous Italian masters of painting despite his youth, moved from his native Umbria to Florence. There he became acquainted with the work of Leonardo who exerted a marked influence on him. The Holy Family, *harmonious, serene and with a light touch of melancholy, shows the Madonna as an ideal of female beauty, in the words of Raphael himself, "a sort of idea", a collective image uniting the features of beautiful faces met by the artist in the course of his life. St Joseph, then customarily depicted as an old bearded man, looks in this painting almost as Raphael's contemporary.*

RAPHAEL (RAFFAELLO SANTI) (1483–1520)
The Conestabile Madonna
Ca. 1503

This small-scale masterpiece created by Raphael in his native Perugia, still bears some traces of the poetic style of Perugino whose pupil the great master was. The artist carefully and lovingly portrayed the details — the face of the beautiful and young Madonna attentively looking into the book, the serious and concentrated Child Christ, the details of the light spring landscape against the background of which the figures are portrayed. The picture was painted on a wooden panel and once it made up a single whole with its frame said to have been produced from a drawing by Raphael.

Titian turned to the image of Danaë, the daughter of Acrisius,
King of Argos, the heroine of an ancient Greek myth, several times.
An oracle prophesied to the king that a son of Danaë would kill him.
Trying to evade death, Acrisius imprisoned Danaë into a brazen
tower and doomed her for lonely life. The beauty, however, was seen

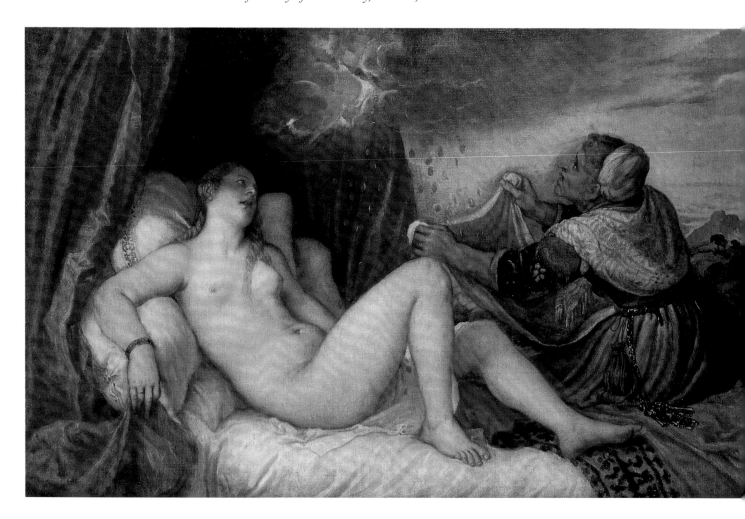

by Zeus, the ruler of the Olympian gods, who, charmed by her
beauty, penetrated to the tower impregnable for mortals in the form
of a shower of gold. Danaë bore Perseus, who later happened
to kill his grandfather.
Titian depicts the culminating moment of the myth — naked
Danaë, reclining on her bed, meets her heavenly lover who
takes the form of the glistening shower of golden coins. The beauty
of Danaë's naked body, combining a perfection of ancient statues
and a truly Venetian stoutness, makes the picture a distinctly
Renaissance hymn to Man, God's most perfect creation.

TITIAN (TIZIANO VECELLIO) (1585/90–1576)
The Repentant Mary Magdalene
1560s

Mary Magdalene is represented in a moment of her passionate prayer. Her eyelids are red
from tears, her eyes are turned upwards, her clothes look like rags. Her image, however, is not an
evocation of an austere asceticism and estranged religious ecstasy. On the contrary, the repentant sinner
is beautiful with an earthly, real beauty. The brush of the great painter conveyed a wealth of shades
of her rich golden hair, the softness of her white skin, the lively gesture of her thin fingers folded in
a gust of prayer. Several wide brushstrokes have been enough to bring out of darkness a crystal vessel.

TITIAN (TITIANO VECELLIO) (1585/90–1576)
St Sebastian
Ca. 1570

St Sebastian *is a masterpiece of Titian's later period. At the moment of his work on the picture he was already about eighty-five, yet the titan of the Renaissance could still paint with a great power and mastery. St Sebastian was one of the most revered saints of the Christian Church in Italy. The young soldier, who preached Christianity, was sentenced to an excruciating torment — he was made an alive target for archers. Traditionally the saint is represented tied to a pole, with dozens of arrows piercing his naked body. Aspiring to God in his prayers, he seems not to feel pain. Titian's treatment does not suggest Christian meekness — St Sebastian, with his powerful and slender body, looks like a hero of Classical Antiquity. It also seems that even the background — the world surrounding the saint — is pervaded with the tragic yet lofty mood of St Sebastian ready to die for the sake of a great idea. The freedom of handling and breadth of expression attained by Titian in this painting are unparalleled in his age, which has led some researchers to think that the canvas is unfinished.*

According to the Gospels, God punished the priest Zacharias, the future father of St John the Baptist, by dumbness because he did not believe that a child could be born of such old parents as he and his wife Elizabeth. Tintoretto, the most prominent Venetian artist of the Late Renaissance, shifted the Gospel scene into a Venetian home filled with servants and wet-nurses bustling around the newly born child. The figures of praying Zacharias, of Elizabeth on her bed, and of the Virgin Mary, who came to visit her relative and herself was already with the Child Christ, are shown in the middle distance.

PAOLO VERONESE (PAOLO CAGLIARI) (1528–1588)
The Lamentation
Between 1576 and 1582

This painting was produced by Paolo Veronese, a well-known Venetian master of the Late Renaissance, for the Church of San Giovanni e Paolo. In the seventeenth century the original was replaced by a copy and sold to a private collection. The representation of the dead Christ in a half-seated posture at the edge of a sarcophagus or on a funeral shroud, had been worked out by Venetian masters as early as the fifteenth century. Veronese's painting, usually marked by bright and saturated colours, filled with dynamism and abundant in personages, is here unusually austere and concise.

The portrait of an unknown man, one of the best examples of this branch of painting, produces an impression of noble dignity, aristocratic ease and subtlety. The exquisite colour scheme based on combinations of silvery, yellow and brown shades, perfectly matches the image of a member of the higher crust of Venetian society portrayed by a leading master of the Venetian school.

Francesco Primaticcio (1504–1570)
*The Holy Family with St Catherine
and St John the Baptist*

Primaticcio was one of the most typical masters of Mannerism, a style popular in Italy in the second half of the sixteenth century. Unlike the harmony and balance which distinguished the painting of the High Renaissance, the art of the Mannerists was characterized by a heightened emotionality, an individual treatment of traditional canonical subjects and a strained dynamism. Figures in Mannerist works were marked by an excessive elongation of proportions and an artificial distortion of shapes, while the colour combinations seemed to be too motley and sharp.

CARAVAGGIO (MICHELANGELO MERISI DA CARAVAGGIO) (1571–1610)
Youth with a Lute. Ca. 1595

This is the only masterpiece by Caravaggio in the Hermitage, which, despite all its seeming realism and genre-like representation of the young musician with a lovely, almost girlish face, has a complex symbolic message. The subject matter of the painting was discussed in numerous investigations which have yielded a number of hypotheses. The most popular concept is that the painting is a version of the vanitas motif meant to remind the spectator of the transience of life. The idea that the youth of the lute player will inevitably pass, is suggested by the broken string of the lute, the flowers which will fade out soon, and the fruit which are to wrinkle and dry out. A different interpretation of the subject is connected with the concept of the five senses. According to this concept, the flowers symbolize smell, the fruit imply taste, the sheets of music refer to eyesight and the sounds of music are a symbol of hearing, while the especial ponderous, three-dimensional quality characteristic of all the details alludes to the sense of touch.

GIOVANNI BATTISTA TIEPOLO
(1696–1770)
*The Triumph
of an Army Leader
Ca. 1720s*

T*he canvas is part of the
series of five large-scale
paintings now in the Hermitage,
created by the outstanding
Venetian painter of the eighteenth century to decorate
the Dolfino Palace in Venice.
The subjects from the history
of ancient Rome borrowed
by Tiepolo from the Roman
*History *by Publius Annius
Florus, were, according to the
painter's views, fine examples
of "a true heroism, loyalty
to one's duty and patriotism".
In* The Triumph of the
Army Leader *pervaded with
dynamism and filled with
numerous figures, the artist
portrays Manius Curius
Dantatus, a Roman army leader
of the third century B.C., who
won a victory over Pyrrhus and
captured elephants as trophy.*

GIORGIO MORANDI (1890–1964)
Metaphysical Still Life
1918

Morandi is one of the most significant and popular Italian artists of the twentieth century, who painted mainly still lifes. His Metaphysical Still Life *dates from the period when Morandi was infatuated with the art of Giorgio de Chirico, who evolved a new painterly metaphysical system, according to which the artist must not reflect the world in the manner of the Impressionists, but to depict only those images which arise from the depth of the subconscious. According to Chirico what is profound is strange and what is strange is unknown and unstudied; so quite really touchable yet as if casually combined objects in the metaphysical still life by Morandi look, in their unusual environment, strange and mysterious.*

POMPEO BORRA (1898–1973)
Nude. 1927

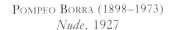

ompeo Borra was active at Milan, a recognized intellectual centre of Italy of the 1920s and 1930s. His smooth and carefully finished works became well-known during the so-called "two black decades" of Mussolini's regime. The leading and officially recognized artistic union Il Novecento, a member of which Borra was, selected Neo-Classicism based on the study and quoting the best examples of great Classical art of the past as the most "Italian" means of self-expression of the contemporary artist.

MASSIMO CAMPIGLI (1895–1971)
Seamstresses
1925

ampigli, a journalist and writer, had no special artistic training. Living in Paris he took an interest in modern art, particularly in Cubist works by Picasso and Léger. On becoming an artist, Campigli sought to reinvigorate the traditions of monumental art combining avant-garde experiments with a profound study of the art of great masters — from paintings on Etruscan sarcophagi to the frescoes of Giotto, Masaccio and Piero della Francesca.

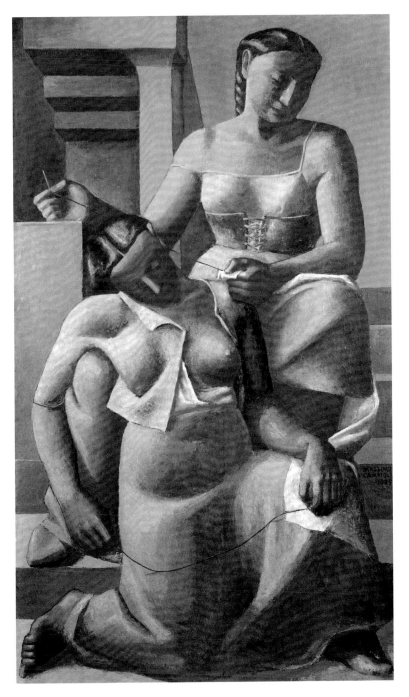

Netherlandish, Flemish & Dutch Painting

15th to 17th Century

T he remarkable collection of seventeenth-century Flemish and Dutch paintings in the Hermitage dates back to long before the museum was founded. In 1716 several hundred paintings arrived in St Petersburg that had been bought for the Tsar in Amsterdam, Brussels and other cities. They were for the most part by Dutch and Flemish artists of whom, according to his biographer, Peter was especially fond. In the first half of the eighteenth century, Flemish and Dutch paintings were eagerly bought for Western European collections too, a number of which Catherine the Great subsequently acquired. The first of these came to Catherine from the Berlin merchant Gotzkowsky in settlement of debts to the Russian treasury. Dutch paintings predominated in it, among them such masterpieces as Jan Steen's *Revellers* and Frans Hals's *Portrait of a Young Man Holding a Glove*. The year 1764, when Gotzkowsky's 225 paintings arrived in St Petersburg, is considered the date of the Hermitage's foundation. In the next twenty years purchases of paintings followed one after another. In Paris in 1766, the Russian ambassador Prince Dmitry Golitsyn, a fine connoisseur of art, acquired for Catherine Rembrandt's monumental canvas *The Return of the Prodigal Son* that came from the collection of Archbishop Clement Augustus of Cologne. Three years later the Hermitage's collection was enlarged by one of the artist's best late portraits, the *Old Man in Red* which arrived as part of the gallery bought in Dresden from the heirs of Count Brühl. This superb quality gallery also contained other Rembrandts, numerous works by the "Small Dutch Masters", and, among its Flemish paintings, such a gem as Rubens's *Perseus and Andromeda*. Particularly rich in masterpieces was the celebrated Crozat collection in Paris that Catherine acquired in 1772. From it come Rembrandt's beautiful *Danaë* and *Holy Family*, an exquisite Van Dyck *Self-Portrait*, Rubens's *Portrait of a Maid of Honour* with its subtle charm, and much else besides. The same high quality marked the Flemish and Dutch canvases in the Walpole collection bought in England a few years later. Particularly valuable in this case were the late portraits by Van Dyck and a series of monumental *Shops* by Frans Snyders.

These acquisitions and others of the late eighteenth century, complemented in 1815 by the Malmaison Gallery which Alexander I bought from Empress Josephine's heirs in Paris, made the Hermitage collection of Flemish and Dutch painting one of the finest in Europe. It acquired tremendous strength in depth a century later, in 1915, with the arrival of more than 700 paintings collected by the Russian scholar and art-lover Piotr Semionov-Tian-Shansky. Along with seventeenth-century works, he also had several by old Netherlandish masters.

Some products of the fifteenth- and sixteenth-century Netherlandish school had already appeared in the Hermitage in Catherine's time, for example, Lucas van Leyden's *Healing of the Blind Man of Jericho* that came from the Crozat collection. Mainly, however, the Netherlandish "primitives" found their way to Russia because of the taste and knowledge of individual nineteenth-century Russian collectors. One of them was the diplomat Dmitry Tatishchev. His collection, the adornment of which was a little diptych by Robert Campin, passed to the Hermitage in 1845 under the owner's will. The history of some paintings is highly unusual. The depiction of *St Luke Painting the Virgin* by the fifteenth-century master Rogier van der Weyden had been cut in two before it reached the Hermitage in two parts, thirty four years apart. The halves were reunited by Hermitage specialists, and so the Virgin "appeared" to St Luke a second time.

Gradually a relatively small, but valuable collection of fifteenth- and sixteenth-century Netherlandish painting formed in the Hermitage. Sadly the Soviet government's sale of museum treasures in the 1920s also affected this part of the gallery. A particularly grievous loss was the only work by Jan van Eyck — the *Annunciation* now in the National Gallery, Washington. At the present time the collection contains more than a hundred works, a considerable number in world terms.

The fifteenth century is justly called the "Golden Age" of Netherlandish painting: it was then that the school formed and had its brilliant heyday. One of its oldest representatives was Robert Campin who is represented in the Hermitage by the altar-piece diptych of *The Trinity* and *The Virgin and Child by the Fireplace* (1430s). Echoes of the Gothic, which continued for a long time in Netherlandish art, combine in his work with a keen interest in worldly reality. That

interest links Campin and his contemporaries to the masters of the Italian Renaissance, although in the fifteenth-century the Low Countries were not yet familiar with the ideas of Humanism. The foundation of their art was a new, pantheistic attitude to the world, as God's beautiful creation, each manifestation of which was worthy of the artist's attention. The paintings of Netherlandish painters are filled with a host of details painted with almost illusory precision, but above all their attraction lies in their glowing colours. Both Campin's diptych and the works by other artists represented in the Hermitage collection were executed in the new technique of oil-painting, the discovery of which was one of the greatest achievements of the Netherlandish school.

In the sixteenth century, thanks to close contacts with Italy and the spread of Humanism, the character of art in the Low Countries changed appreciably: new genres appeared, works on traditional Christian subjects took on an ever-increasing secular character, but even then the artists retained a vivid identity of their own. This is evident in the work of the greatest artists of that time: Pieter Bruegel the Elder and Lucas van Leyden. The latter is represented in the Hermitage by one of his finest works, the 1531 triptych *The Healing of the Blind Man of Jericho*.

By the beginning of the seventeenth century, the Netherlandish artistic school had ceased to exist as a single whole, and the country itself had lost its former unity. After a long struggle with Spain, that had ruled the Low Countries since the middle of the sixteenth century, the seven northern provinces became the independent Dutch state. In the south, known as Flanders after the largest province, Spanish regents retained control. Both countries were famed for their artistic schools and they are represented in the Hermitage by large collections of superb quality.

The brilliant flourishing of Flemish painting in the first half of the seventeenth century is connected above all with the name of Peter Paul Rubens. As head of the national school, he decisively transformed art in his country and gave it a new direction. The about forty works by Rubens in the Hermitage — altarpieces, "mythologies" and allegories, portraits, landscapes and sketches for decorative series — give an idea of the great, many-sided talent of the artist and of various periods in his career.

The early works, full of impressions of the art of the Ancient World and the Renaissance which Rubens studied during his time in Italy, already display the artist's profound individuality: his personages embody a purely Flemish ideal of full-blooded beauty and vitality. Such energetic images impressed his countrymen who dreamt of the regeneration of a Flanders exhausted by the long war. The natural expression of Rubens's temperament and world-view was the Baroque style, of which he was one of the active creators. Among the masterpieces of the European Baroque is the painting *Perseus and Andromeda*, painted about 1622 when Rubens's skill as a painter attained a special brilliance. Works like this with their captivating impetuous energy and vivid colours are typical for the artist's mature period, from which most of the Hermitage's works belong. But in the Hermitage it is also possible to discover a totally different side to Rubens. The *Portrait of a Maid of Honour* (about 1625) is one of the artist's unique paintings. Devoid of showy effects and austere in its colour scheme, it tells of Rubens's ability to profoundly sense the inner life of his model, conveying the subtlest psychological nuances.

The distinguishing feature of the Hermitage's Flemish collection, which numbers more than 500 paintings, lies in the fact that the school's leading figures are represented by a large number of works, as a rule of differing character. Twenty-four paintings by Anthony van Dyck, who was famed as the best portraitist in Europe while still young, demonstrate various facets of his talent. He appears to the viewer as a deep psychologist, the author of striking formal portraits of monarchs and aristocrats, and as the creator of charming images of children, but first and foremost as an outstanding painter. A particularly fine colour scheme distinguishes the portraits of his

"English period", which is well represented in the Hermitage. They were painted in the 1630s, the last decade of Van Dyck's short life, when he worked in London at the court of Charles I.

Rubens's studio, where Van Dyck worked as a young man, was the centre of all artistic life in Flanders. Many talented painters worked together there, recruited by Rubens to satisfy large commissions. For many years Frans Snyders too was associated with the studio. That artist

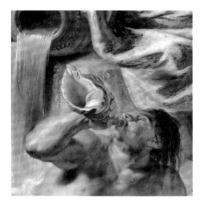

attained particular fame with the *Shops* series now in the Hermitage, consisting of four huge canvases painted to adorn the bishop's dining-room in Bruges. No other European school in the seventeenth century produced anything like these monumental still lifes in which, it seems, all nature's rich bounty is assembled. The distinctive quality of Flemish art is no less vividly revealed in the works of Jacob Jordaens, especially in the best known of his Hermitage paintings, *The Bean King* which depicts a popular national custom. Works of the "Rubensian tendency" comprise the most valuable part of the Flemish collection, but other artists are well represented, in particular the masters of "cabinet painting". Noteworthy here is the collection of paintings by David Teniers the Younger who was a great success with the European public in the second half of the seventeenth century: it numbers about fifty works of different genres and is considered the finest in the world.

The Dutch school formed later than the Flemish — by the 1630s, and its heyday came in the middle of that century. Nowhere else outside the Netherlands is that school so fully represented as in the Hermitage. It is not merely a question of the size of the collection (more than 1,000 paintings!) and the abundance of masterpieces — the great masters appear here together with a host of lesser artists whose works are at times rarities even in Dutch collections. This quality of the Hermitage collection reflects the actual situation that arose in middle-class Protestant Holland in the seventeenth century: in no other country in Europe at that time was there such an enormous number of artists, and nowhere was painting so closely bound up with people's everyday lives. The overwhelming majority of the artists (known as "the Small Dutch Masters") painted small-scale works suitable for the modestly sized rooms of the burghers' homes, preferring to depict scenes from the daily existence of contemporaries, their appearance and possessions, the nature and towns of their native land. The "art of reality" — the portrait, landscape, still life and genre scenes — became highly developed in Holland and had a pronounced national character. Among the Small Dutch Masters were such talented painters as Steen, Pieter de Hooch, Ter Borch, Kalf and Emanuel de Witte, who are represented in the Hermitage by superb works. Against this background a few great masters stand out whose work is marked

by especial depth and scale. There is the outstanding portraitist Frans Hals, represented in the museum by two excellent late portraits, the philosophical landscape painter Jacob van Ruisdael, eleven of whose works belong to the Hermitage, and finally Holland's greatest artist Rembrandt van Rijn.

The Hermitage's collection of his works can without exaggeration be called unique. More than twenty paintings (some possibly executed in part by pupils) trace the complicated path followed by the master across four decades: from the early works still executed in the traditional Dutch manner that brought him success with the public to the philosophically profound and tragic late images that found understanding only among rare sympathizers. *Danaë*, *The Holy Family* and *David and Uriah*, created in different years, are milestone works for Rembrandt, reflecting his understanding of life and work. At the same time these masterpieces demonstrate the distinctive artistic idiom that in his mature period set him apart from his Dutch contemporaries. About half the Hermitage's Rembrandts are portraits and among them the late depictions of elderly people stand out for their psychological complexity. An entirely special place in Rembrandt's legacy is occupied by the monumental canvas from his last years *The Return of the Prodigal Son*, a brilliant summary of his thoughts on the meaning of life and the highest manifestation of his mastery as a painter.

Netherlands

ROBERT CAMPIN
(CA. 1380–1444)
*The Virgin and Child
at the Fireplace*
1430s

Campin's composition is the
right-hand part of a miniature
diptych the left wing of which
represents the Holy Trinity.
The intimate world of the
Infant Christ is interpreted
here as a scene in a contemporary
burgher home, with characteristic furnishings of the period.
The Virgin is given a typically
Netherlandish features. Each
detail is lovingly portrayed.
Campin renders with great
mastery a diffused daylight
sliding along the walls and
playing with reflections
on the metal household wares.
The subtlety of treatment which
distinguishes this picture, the
earliest piece of oil painting
in the Hermitage collection,
endows it with a special
verisimilitude characteristic
of Netherlandish art dating
from the age of the Renaissance.
At the same time many details
imply a symbolic meaning:
the washstand and towel, for
example, symbolize the purity
of St Mary, while the sky in
the window above the Child's
head alludes to the invisible
presence of God.

ROGIER VAN DER WEIDEN (CA. 1400–1464)
St Luke Painting the Virgin
1430s

Legend has it that St Luke was the first artist who painted the earliest portrait of the Virgin
when She was appearing to him with the Child in Her arms. Painters regarded St Luke as their
heavenly patron and not infrequently endowed his representations in their paintings with lifelike
features as did Rogier van der Weiden here. His composition is characteristic of Netherlandish
art: the figures in the foreground are placed so as they would not obstruct the space unfolding in the
vista between the columns. History and everyday life, man and nature are blended in this painting
to form a many-sided image of the earthly living.

LUCAS VAN LEYDEN (1489 OR 1494 – 1533)
The Healing of the Blind Man of Jericho
Triptych. 1531

This triptych altarpiece was painted by Lucas van Leyden for a chapel of the hospital in his native Leyden — that is why he chose a Gospel scene of Christ healing the blind man in the environs of Jericho. The artist enjoyed a great popularity in the sixteenth century and his name was lauded in verses. Lucas van Leyden is at his best in this painting, with a bright, vivid colour scheme, a motley crowd of people shown against the background of a landscape, and the figures of heralds on the side wings.

Flanders

PETER PAUL RUBENS (1577–1640)
Perseus and Andromeda
Ca. 1622

A myth about Perseus, a hero who vanquished the Gorgon Medusa and saved the beautiful Andromeda *from the sea monster, was one of Rubens's favourite subjects to which he turned several times. The dynamic composition of the painting characteristic of the Baroque style, combines heroic and lyrical motifs. The bright, contrasting spots of colour have an optimistic resonance; the young girl's body is painted in translucent soft shades and the overall chromatic scheme is built up of the subtlest nuances of colour.*

The immediate reason for the creation of this painting was the blockade of the estuary of the Scheldt River on which Antwerp stands, by Dutch ships. The Flemish master expressed in an allegorical form a hope that "these lands will again flourish" as soon as they would have an access to the sea. But as is usual with Rubens, his allegory also has a more general, global meaning.

PETER PAUL RUBENS
(1577–1640)
Roman Charity
1612

This painting produced by
Rubens soon after his return
from Italy, reflects his impression of Classical art—
the composition with the two
large figures in the foreground
has been inspired by ancient
reliefs, while the powerful old
man is reminiscent of Michelangelo's heroes. The subject
of this work was borrowed
from a book by the Roman
writer Valerius Maximus and
illustrates an example of self-
denying love. It depicts a young
woman on a visit to her father
in a dungeon. She is suckling the
weakened man to save him from
an imminent death of hunger.

PETER PAUL RUBENS (1577–1640)
Portrait of the Maid of Honour
Ca. 1625

The title of this amazingly subtle portrait is related to the inscription on the preliminary drawing The Infanta's Waiting-Maid
in Brussels *dating from the seventeenth century, although
not a work by Rubens. The name of the heroine is not known.
There is a surmise that this is an imaginary portrait of Rubens's
daughter Clara Serena, who died at twelve, painted several
years after her death.*

FRANS SNYDERS (1579–1657)
Fruit Shop
Ca. 1618–20

Thisslarge-scale canvas, together with three similar paintings, depicting a vegetable, fish and game shops, makes up a picturesque ensemble created for the decoration of the state Dining Room in the house of Archbishop Anthony at Brugge. Although Snyders specialized in depicting fruit and various food, he rarely painted intimate pictures and it was due to this reason that he was named the "Rubens of still life". His huge, sweeping and dynamic works symbolize a dream of the artist's compatriots about the Flemish "Golden Age". It seems that the traditional French word nature morte is hardly appropriate here — the paintings show not a dead life, but living nature, the abundant and flowering world, endlessly rich and generous.

JACOB JORDAENS (1593–1678)
The Bean King
Ca. 1638

"The feast of the bean king" was celebrated in Flanders on 6 January and was one of the most popular festivals. During that day a large pie was baked in every home, with a bean put inside. The one who would find the bean in his piece of pie, was honoured as the "king" of the holiday. A "queen" and a "suite" were chosen for him from among the guests and when he lifted his goblet, everybody was supposed to shout in chorus: "The king is drinking!" and immediately empty his goblet to escape a joking fine. Jordaens devoted to this subject a lot of paintings which have revealed the Flemings' live-asserting characters. The Hermitage's Bean King, remarkable for its composition and colourful figures of drinking people, is one of Jordaens's indubitable masterpieces.

This is the most famous self-portrait by Van Dyck featuring him at the age of twenty-eight. The skilfully rendered painting has preserved the freshness and immediacy of a sketch from nature. The artist succeeded in attaining the richest pictorial effect by means of the "simplest" colours — white, black and grey.

ANTHONY VAN DYCK (1599– 1641)
Portrait of Philadelphia and Elizabeth Wharton
Late 1630s

The double portrait of the girls reveals another facet of Van Dyck's talent — his ability to convey the entire freshness and naivety of the childish perception of the world without any sentimentality. The small Philadelphia and Elizabeth vividly and naturally play the roles of society ladies before the viewer. The cold silvery tones form an exquisite colour range which would serve as a source of inspiration for eighteenth-century English painters.

ANTHONY VAN DYCK (1599– 1641)
Family Portrait
1621

Rubens was the first who appreciated Van Dyck's talent as a portrait painter; so it was he and his friends who commissioned first portraits from the young artist. The *Family Portrait* probably features the well-known Flemish portraitist Jan Wildens. The inspired face with a pensive look suggests a subtle creative personality, while the appearance of his wife reveals her earthly predilections. The childish figure with a funny round face seems to unite her parents emphasizing the stability of their union.

Brower was one of the most unusual and talented painters of Flanders. Trained in the workshop of Frans Hals in Holland, he could combine in his small-scale paintings the subtlety in conveying the light-and-air medium, characteristic of the Dutch masters, with an open emotionality inherent to his fellow-countrymen. The themes of his paintings were sharply differing from those of the Rubens circle — he always preferred to represent the lower classes and outcasts of society.

JAN BREUGHEL
(THE VELVET BREUGHEL)
(1568–1625)
Edge of a Forest
1610

Jan Breughel, generally known as the Velvet Breughel, the younger son of the great painter of the Renaissance Pieter Breughel, was a recognized master of "study painting" in the early seventeenth century. His small-scale pictures, pre-eminently landscapes and flower compositions, striking for their minute attention to detail and elaborate finish, enjoyed a great success with European art collectors.

The legacy of Teniers is marked by a great variety of genres in which he worked. Among his paintings in the Hermitage there are many everyday scenes. His Peasant Wedding is like an unhurried detailed story in which a special attention is paid to the details of the peasant costumes, country houses and scenery, while the people he depicts look like amateurish actors performing a merry play.

Holland

JAN STEEN (1625/26–1679)
The Revellers
Ca. 1660

A gambler and amateur actor, Steen often depicted himself in his paintings. Here he "plays a role" of a careless lower-class reveller, merry-making in the company of his girl-friend. The fire going out and a mess in the room emphasize the unduly mode of life of the heroes. One of Steen's masterpieces, this painting is remarkable for its perfectly arranged composition and subtle colour scheme with the expressive highlights of red and yellow.

EMANUEL DE WITTE (1616/17–1692)
Interior of a Church
1671

A problem of rendering atmospheric effects was one of central in Dutch art of the seventeenth century. It attracted not only landscape and genre painters, but also still-life artists. Moreover, it even brought to life a special form of art known as interior painting, which was practiced, among others, by the eminent painter Emanuel de Witte. He painted church interiors using as a rule real life models. In the Hermitage picture he combined the features of the Old and New Churches of Amsterdam. But it is not the architectural monument that especially interests him, but the complex space articulated by the powerful columns and arches and filled with a vivid play of light penetrating from different sources. The contrasts of blinding spots of sunlight and black shadows introduce a tension and dynamism into the picture.

GERARD TER BORCH (1617–1681)
A Glass of Lemonade
1660s

This is one of the most brilliant works by Ter Borch, who ranks among the best genre painters of the Dutch school. With great skill the artist conveyed here not only the texture of fabrics with a rich play of light reflexes, but also an expressive "dialogue" of glances and gestures between the young lady and her cavalier. The old woman standing next to them probably is not as innocent as it might seem at first sight, for one of the most popular subjects of the Small Dutch Masters were scenes with a procuress.

WILLEM CLAESZ HEDA (1594–1680/82)
Breakfast with Lobster
1648

The seventeenth century saw a rapid development of the still life in Holland
as nowhere else. This kind of painting had different features in every city. The artists
of Utrecht, for example, preferred to paint flowers, in The Hague they depicted sea gifts
and in Leyden, a university centre, "philosophical" still lifes were in vogue. Especially
popular were so-called "breakfast" scenes. Heda was one of those who evolved this
kind of still life which became a classical one for the Dutch school. It seems that a
man has just left the table depicted in the painting and all the objects portrayed still
retain the traces of his touches. Their seemingly casual disposition conceals the artist's
subtle calculation — contrasting in shapes and texture, the objects highlight one
another and at the same time make up a pictorial unity full of harmony and balance.

A brilliant painter of the Dutch school during its heyday, Kalf had no rivals in the art of translating the prose of material objects into a poetic language of painting. Like a fairy-tale knight, a gilded cup towers in the centre of the table above other objects. The wealth of the palette, the contrasts of light and shade are combined in Kalf's still lifes with a luxury of the objects, which became an indispensable part of everyday life in the second half of the seventeenth century.

GABRIEL METSU (1629–1667)
The Doctor's Visit
1660s

A doctor's visit was a subject popular in Dutch painting under the influence of the theatre. Many artists, following the authors of stage performances, treated them in a humorous vein, representing women suffering from "love disease" incurable by any doctor. Metsu seems to keep a serious tone in the Hermitage piece, yet the very composition showing a woman with a pale face seated in an armchair, with her maid and a physician standing nearby, is built according to the principles of the theatrical mise-en-scène.

Man and his environment harmoniously coexist in the painting arranged by the artist as a window to the world of well-being and order. In the foreground is a terrace where the mistress gives orders to her maid, behind her unfolds a brick-paved yard; through the arch can be seen an embankment — the space itself suggests a quiet, slow rhythm of life dominating the scene.

FRANS HALS (1581/85–1666)
Portrait of a Young Man Holding a Glove
Ca. 1650

During his long creative career Hals seemed to portray entire
Holland, from authoritative burghers and scholars to peasants and
tramps. But whoever his heroes are, they are never reserved, but enter
an unconstrained contact with viewers. The figure of the young man
is shifted to the edge of the canvas so that it seems to have just noticed
us — his eyes have glistened and a slight smile has appeared on his lips
and his hand holding a glove sliding down has stiffened for a moment.

WILLEM DUYSTER (CA. 1599–1635)
Officers in a Guard-House
Ca. 1633

Paintings by Dutch artists often show military people. This is not surprising for the country which recently led a heroic war for its liberation. However, officers and soldiers are represented not in the heat of battle scenes but at rest. In this painting, two of them are playing cards in the depth of the room and smoking pipes in a candle light, while two others are warming themselves and listening to stories told by their friend, a young man with a fairly exotic appearance. Perhaps he tells them about foreign lands — the Dutchmen used to sail all around the world in those days. The sharp contrasts of the black silhouettes and the bright spots of light conjure up a special, somewhat mysterious atmosphere in the foreground...

JAN PORCELLIS
(CA. 1584–1632)
Ships at Sea on a Rough Day

Very patriotically inclined, the Dutch painters loved the unassuming, modest nature of their motherland, observing it in various seasons and in different weather conditions. Their landscapes are invariably concrete and yet filled with emotions. Porcellis was one of the first marine painters of the Dutch school. The seascape was for him primarily the water and sky combined by the wet atmosphere saturated with light. His depictions of ships merely enhance this impression of the motion of the air and water.

REMBRANDT VAN RIJN (1606–1669)
Flora
1634

This picture painted by Rembrandt soon after he married Saskia van Uylenburgh
is a sort of memorial to their love. The artist's young wife is represented as the
ancient goddess of spring and gardens. Dressed in a luxurious old-fashioned garment
and crowned with a lavish spray of flowers, with a staff in her hand, Saskia
is portrayed in a shaded grotto and seems to be a little embarrassed by the role
she has to play at the will of her husband. This gives her image a deeply sincere
and emotional note.

REMBRANDT VAN RIJN (1606–1669)
Danaë
1636–42

The subject of this famous painting was based on an ancient Greek myth popular in European art — Danaë was imprisoned by his father in a tower and doomed for eternal solitude, but Zeus, attracted by her beauty, penetrated to her in the form of a golden shower. Rembrandt presents the heroine of the ancient myth primarily as an earthly woman, emphasizing the charming timidity with which she is waiting for her divine lover. The light pouring in from the depth of the picture, suggests the arrival of Zeus and creates a glistening atmosphere around her.

Rembrandt's work was distinguished not only for its wide scope
— he worked in different genres and painted both monumental
and intimate pictures. However, everyday scenes, so popular
with his beloved "Small Dutch Masters", are quite rare in
his work. This small-scale canvas in the Hermitage collection
is one of such paintings. It seems to be executed in a single sitting,
in a wide, nearly sketchy manner characteristic of his later period.

REMBRANDT VAN RIJN (1606–1669)
The Holy Family
1645

In the 1640s, after the death of his beloved
wife, one of Rembrandt's favourite subjects was
the Holy Family in which perhaps his dream
of the lost home was realized. In the Hermitage
painting the artist has found the deepest and
most expressive solution of this subject. Light
becomes with Rembrandt not only a physical
but also a spiritual phenomenon. In its stream
are hovering the Angels, it comes from the fire
symbolizing the homely hearth, it illuminates
the cradle of the Infant Christ and the face
of the Virgin Mary, it glistens on the pages
of the Bible. The light is treated here as a symbol
of life, love and wisdom.

REMBRANDT VAN RIJN (1606–1669)
Portrait of an Old Man in Red
1652–54

In the 1640s the work of Rembrandt began to lose its popularity with burgher society. The numerous portraits dating from his later period were mainly not commissions but works he painted for himself. His models were people close to him or unknown inhabitants of the outskirts of Amsterdam. The old man, shown seated quietly in an armchair with his tired hands resting on his lap, seems to be absorbed in thoughts and recollections. It is not by chance that such later psychological portraits by Rembrandt became known as "portraits-biographies".

REMBRAND VAN RIJN ((1606–1669)
David and Uriah
1663–65

Rembrandt's later paintings on Biblical subjects are distinguished by their extremely concise treatment — they have no outer action and details of the setting are nearly absent. Represented in close-up is Uriah slowly moving towards the viewer. He is being sent to death by King David, who has fallen in love with his wife Bathsheba. The king shown behind his back seems already to begin to repent the evil he did, and the face of the elderly scribe bespeaks deep sorrow. The hero is outwardly restrained, but the strong shadow covering his face and the turbulent, seemingly exploding red colour of his garment are evocative of his dark presentiment.

REMBRANDT VAN RIJN
(1606–1669)
Return of the Prodigal Son
Ca. 1663–65

The Gospel parable of the reckless son attracted many European artists. Rembrandt represented the end of the story — a return of the repentant sinner to his father's home. The huge canvas, similar to an altarpiece, has nothing extraneous about it; even its colour and light and the pictorial surface itself have acquired a somewhat spiritual quality.

Spanish
Painting *15th to 19th Century*

I nterest in Spanish painting really started in Europe in the early nineteenth century, after the Napoleonic Wars, when the works of the greatest artists hitherto kept in the monasteries, cathedrals and palaces of Spain began to appear at auctions in Paris and London. It was then that the Hermitage formed its relatively small (some 150 works), but, in comparison with other museums around the world, fairly full collection of Spanish painting, mainly from the seventeenth century. The beginning, however, goes back to Catherine the Great. Eighteenth-century collectors, if they were interested in Spanish art, preferred Murillo, and so his works appeared almost immediately after the foundation of the picture gallery — in 1768 *The Rest on the Flight into Egypt*; in 1771 *Boy with a Dog* and its pendant *Girl with Fruit* (now in the Pushkin Museum in Moscow). Several first-rate seventeenth-century Spanish works came with the Walpole collection, including Murillo's monumental *Immaculate Conception*, erroneously known in England as *The Ascension of the Virgin*. From an unspecified collection sometime before 1774 the Hermitage acquired its Velázquez *Luncheon*, then considered to be by an unknown Flemish artist.

In 1810–11, the Hermitage gained two more superb Murillos, dating from the highest point of his career — *The Blessing of Jacob* and *Jacob's Dream*, belonging to a four-picture series on the life of the Old Testament patriarch. They were acquired specially for the Hermitage collection by Baron Dominique-Vivant Denon, the Director General of the Museums of France and advisor to Napoleon, who had been secretary of the French embassy in St Petersburg durings the reign of Catherine the Great.

An important event was the acquisition in 1814 of the collection of the Amsterdam banker Coesevelt who had bought up paintings at minimal prices in impoverished post-war Spain. The purchase brought some real gems — Velázquez's *Portrait of Olivares*, Zurbarán's *Girlhood of the Madonna*, and works by Morales, Pantoja de la Cruz, Ribalta, and others.

In the nineteenth century paintings by Ribera, Zurbarán, Cano and Murillo arrived with the collections of Napoleon's first wife Josephine Beauharnais, the Spanish minister Manuel de Godoy, and others. Individual masterpieces also came from auctions. For example, the noted Russian academic painter and director of the Academy of Arts, Fiodor Bruni, bought in Paris in 1852 Zurbarán's unique monumental depiction of St Lawrence.

By the beginning of the twentieth century collectors were turning their eyes beyond the celebrated masters of the seventeenth century to earlier artists whose work had until then been considered insufficiently accomplished. A real sensation was caused by the discovery in the Russian capital of a painting by El Greco. The work was in the collection of General Durnovo, but, although it is signed, the military man had no idea of its real value. *The Apostles Peter and Paul* was a revelation at the portrait exhibition organized in 1908 by the periodical *Stariye Gody*. In 1911 the owner presented it to the Hermitage.

The Spanish collection continued to expand after 1917 as well, chiefly due to the nationalization of private collections. Finally, in 1974, the noted American collector Armand Hammer presented the Hermitage with the *Portrait of the Actress Antonia Zárate* by Goya, a great master who was not represented in the museum. Goya is considered the last outstanding Spanish artist to have worked in his homeland. In the nineteenth century artists were obliged to leave a country that had become a second-rate cultural hinterland. The Hermitage does have a few works by Spanish artists of the period, most notably Mariano Fortuny and Ignacio Zuloaga, fashionable salon painters in late-nineteenth-century Paris. The great Spaniard of the twentieth-century, Pablo Picasso, arrived in Paris at the beginning of the twentieth century as an eighteen-year old youth and all his life was connected with French art. His work therefore properly belongs to France.

Spanish painting developed in its own special way, different from neighbouring European countries. The year 1492 saw the final victory over the Moors who had conquered the greater part of the Iberian peninsula almost eight hundred years before. By the early sixteenth century Spain, having gained the New World and some countries in North Africa, part of Italy and the Netherlands, had turned into a very rich state. It did not flourish for long, however. By the beginning of the next century the economic boom was a thing of the past. The sixteenth century saw the beginning of the Renaissance period in Spanish culture. In painting the leading genre was religious pictures. Probably the most significant artist, typically Spanish in spirit, was Luis de Morales who created profoundly dramatic, at times tragically ecstatic depictions of the Virgin Mary. The formal portrait, strictly regulated in terms of the devices used, was the sole secular genre. In the Hermitage works by Alonso Sanchez Coello and his pupil Juan Pantoja de la Cruz give an idea of the aristocratic refinement and noble restraint of the best examples of the genre.

The "Golden Age" of Spanish painting is generally held to be the seventeenth century. It opened, though, with Cretan-born Domenicos Theotocopoulos, who arrived in Spain from Italy back in the 1570s, and achieved greatness and fame under the nickname El Greco. The Hermitage has two works by him. The portrait of the sixteenth-century poet Alonso de Ercilla y Zuñiga, author of the celebrated epic poem *La Araucana*, came from the Coesevelt collection and was apparently produced before his move to Spain. The other painting is world famous — *The Apostles Peter and Paul*, first of a series devoted to Christ and the disciples that the artist produced when already in Toledo.

Among the highest achievements of Spanish seventeenth-century painting are the works of Diego Velázquez, José de Ribera, Francisco de Zurbarán and Bartolomé Esteban Murillo.

Six paintings by Ribera begin the display. This artist worked almost all his life in Naples, then part of the kingdom of Spain. A typical Spanish artist, religious and sincere to the point of exaltation, he absorbed all the best that the Italian school of painting could offer. The brilliant work of Caravaggio served as the source for a manner of painting which then influenced Ribera's compatriots. His religious paintings look like dramatic real-life scenes, full of contrasts of light and shade, in which real-life Spaniards live and suffer. The Hermitage depictions of martyr-saints are among the artist's acknowledged masterpieces.

The work of Velázquez, Spain's foremost artist, the court painter to Phillip IV, is represented in the Hermitage by two paintings. *Luncheon*, an early work by the eighteen-year-old painter, belongs to the *bodegón* ("tavern") genre exceptionally common in Spain. The portrait of the Count-Duke of Olivares, all powerful minister at the royal court and the artist's exalted patron, is among the undoubted masterpieces of Velázquez's work in this field.

Zurbarán worked all his life in the Andalusian capital Seville, a very important cultural centre for the country. His religious paintings adorned numerous Sevillian churches and monasteries. Few works by this major artist have left his homeland. The Hermitage has four. *The Girlhood of the Madonna* is one of the few small-scale lyrical paintings in a generally austere, emotionally restrained oeuvre. By contrast, *St Lawrence*, painted for the St Joseph Monastery in Seville, is striking for its monumental size, and the figure of the saint, holding the instrument of his martyrdom — a gridiron on which he was roasted, seems to grow out of the earth, almost a three-dimensional statue precisely drawn against an immense bright sky.

The works of the last Golden Age master, Murillo, were, as has been said, the most popular with collectors and for that reason the Hermitage has a considerable number — seventeen, reflecting all stages of his career. *Boy with a Dog* dates from his early period, which was dominated by vivid images of little waifs, gypsies and beggars dressed in picturesque rags, who never loose the immediate expression of feelings that goes with their age.

The great Francisco Goya, whose work around the turn of the nineteenth century marked the end of the heyday of Spanish painting, is represented in the Hermitage collection by the *Portrait of the Actress Antonia Zárate*. This emotional, moving image of a young woman, a "portrait of the heart" in the words of one scholar, is a sort of link between two eras in painting — the passing age of great spiritual revelations, of Goya's beloved Velázquez and Rembrandt, and the dawning age of Romanticism.

Juan Pantoja de la Cruz, court painter to the Kings Philip II and Philip III, was active in Madrid and the royal residence at El Escorial. He painted numerous portraits of representatives of the haughty and proud Spanish aristocracy — the seemingly immobile flat figures clad in luxurious garments and decorated with orders and gems against a dark background. Diego di Villamayor belonged to the celebrated aristocratic family founded as early as the eleventh century. The Order of the Alcantara which could be worn only by the selected few suggests the noble origin of the seventeen-year-old grandee.

LUIS DE MORALES
(BETWEEN 1520 AND 1525–1585)
The Madonna and Child

The vivid expressiveness and tragic exaltation of religious paintings by Morales are connected with the artist's world view which was formed under the influence of mysticism, widespread in certain circles of Spanish sixteenth-century society that repudiated the role of the Church as a mediator between the believer and God. This trend was severely persecuted by the Inquisition and Morales's paintings, with their free interpretation of religious subjects, failed to won recognition at the Spanish court. The artist spent most of his life in the provincial Badajoz, the capital of Estremadur.

EL GRECO
(DOMENIKOS THEOTOKOPULOS)
(1541–1614)
The Apostles Peter and Paul

According to the Scriptures, the characters of St Peter and St Paul, Christ's pupils, were quite opposite. The picture by El Greco is perhaps based on the Gospel scene illustrating the only conflict between the two Apostles when the resolute and undaunted St Paul rebuked the meek St Peter for his inconsistency revealed during their conversion of pagans to Christianity at Antioch.

DIEGO VELÁZQUEZ (1599–1660)
Luncheon
Ca. 1617–18

At first sight, the artist depicts a tavern scene with real Spanish people shown seated at a modest meal, illuminated by a narrow stream of direct light in the manner of Caravaggio, which emphasizes them against the semi-dark background. Velázquez invests this seemingly everyday scene, in the same way as Caravaggio did, with some additional meaning. The still-life objects in the foreground — a pomegranate, a loaf and a glass of wine — are Christian symbols and the images of the boy, youth and old man can be related to the three periods in human life.

DIEGO VELÁZQUEZ (1599–1660)
Portrait of Count-Duke of Olivares
Ca. 1640

Don *Gaspar de Guzmán, Count of Olivares, Duke of San Lucár,
became the mighty Prime-Minister since the moment when the sixteen-
year-old Philip IV ascended the throne. The clever, sly, well educated
and energetic Olivares concentrated all power in his hands. It was
thanks to him that Velázquez received the position of count painter.
Velázquez did not idealize the appearance of his patron of elevated
rank. The portrait, very simple and austere in composition, reflexes
the complicated, tragically contradictory character of the factual ruler
of Spain who would have to spend the end of his life in exile.*

FRANCISCO DE ZURBARÁN (1598–1664)
St Laurent
1636

Legend has it that St Laurent was the first deacon of the Roman Christian Church. Enemies burnt him on an iron gridiron which became a symbol of the saint used in his numerous depictions. Zurbarán, following the Spanish tradition, endows the image with distinctive individual features. It is known that the painter used for the painting a representation of a common monk whose appearance could hardly be described as heroic. However, Zurbarán created a devotional painting marked by an air of monumentality and significance.

FRANCISCO DE ZURBARÁN
(1598–1664)
The Girlhood of the Madonna
Ca. 1660

The Girlhood of the Madonna *was one of Zurbarán's favourite subjects. His Virgin Mary, a black-haired and dark-eyed Spanish girl illuminated by a powerful stream of light pouring from above, seems to stiffen in a deep and silent ecstasy of prayer. Even this small and intimate work by Zurbarán is marked by a monumental quality inherent to his work.*

BARTOLOMÉ ESTEBAN MURILLO (1617–1682)
Boy with a Dog
1650s

S*pecialists single out three periods in the work of the celebrated
Murillo— the* estile frio *("cold"), the* estile calido *("warm")
and the* estile vaporoso *("airy"). The* Boy with a Dog *dates from
the early period when the artist worked in the* estile frio *and eagerly
painted common people, tramps, gypsies and beggars clad in picturesque rags, who were poor yet optimistic and ingenious in revealing
their feelings. The light colour scheme used by Murillo in such
paintings gave the name to this period of his work.*

Francisco Goya (1746–1828)
Portrait of of the Actress Antonia Zárate
Ca. 1811

Antonia Zárate was born in a famous family
of actors. She made her debut as an actress
in Madrid at the end of the eighteenth century.
Probably she was more popular for her
fascinating beauty than for her talent, and if
Goya would not have left two splendid portraits
of her (the second likeness is in a private collection in Ireland), her name would not have
reached us. It is exactly known who commissioned the portrait of the actress. Goya often
attended performances in the theatre where
Antonia performed together with her husband
and sister and he knew many actors. The portrait
could be commissioned from the artist by Manuel
Garsia de la Prada, a member of the municipal
assembly of Madrid, who was a close friend and
patron of the actress. She died of tuberculosis
at the age of thirty-six.

Antonio Pereda (1608–1678)
Still Life
1652

Spanish artists invested the still life, which occupied
a prominent place in national art, with their admiration
of the beauty and harmonious orderliness of things created
by human hands. Pereda seems to carefully touch every
object in his still life delighting in the transparency of glass,
density and brightness of painted earthenware pottery and
the glitter of metal vessel for boiling coffee, comparing
their texture with biscuits and cheese in the foreground
which add a sense of invisible human presence into
a realm of "dead nature".

German
Painting *15th to 20th Century*

Almost five centuries of German painting — from the late fifteenth to the middle of the twentieth — are represented in the Hermitage. This collection is of considerable size (some 700 paintings), although less comprehensive than others in the museum. Its composition is to a large extent due to how it formed.

The section opens with the Renaissance period, a brief, but vivid flourishing of German art in the work of Dürer and his contemporaries. Most precious here are the paintings of Lucas Cranach the Elder, one of the outstanding artists of the first half of the sixteenth century. Three of them — *Venus and Cupid*, *Portrait of a Woman* and *The Virgin and Child under the Apple-Tree* — are among his masterpieces. They convey the profound originality of German art in an age in which the ideas of Humanism combined with the religious spirit of the Reformation. This gives, for example, a special colouring to Cranach's mythological images. Interest in the real world, founded on a pantheistic attitude, expresses itself in the artist's careful attention to detail and his splendid landscape backgrounds. A fine feeling for nature was common to many German artists and it is not surprising that in this period, together with Holland, Germany produced a new genre — landscape.

German achievements in the field of portraiture at that time were particularly significant. They are represented by the works of various artists, including Ambrosius Holbein. This talented painter and graphic artist, brother of the famous Hans Holbein the Younger, died at the age of twenty-four and his works are a great rarity even in German museums. Altogether the Hermitage collection has only a few dozen works from the Renaissance and lacks the comprehensiveness that might be wished. In this it is, however, not an exception among museums outside Germany.

Before the twentieth century, Russian and most European collectors had no real interest in the old German masters. The only exceptions were Dürer and Holbein, to whom works by other artists were often attributed. In 1838, for example, the Hermitage supposedly had eight Dürers and eight Holbeins, none of which actually belonged to them. Renaissance paintings, although they came to St Petersburg mainly in the eighteenth century, some as part of the large collections Catherine the Great bought, were still rare and not the object of special collection. There was a little interest too in the German art of the seventeenth century, which in general was considerably poorer than that of other countries. The isolated gifted Germany artists of that period represented in the Hermitage studied and worked mainly outside their native country and were associated with the leading European schools, Dutch, Flemish and Italian, preferred by eighteenth-century collectors.

At the same time, from Peter the Great's reign, there was great interest in Russia in contemporary German art buoyed up by ties of politics and kinship between the Russian and German courts. Catherine actively acquired works by then-fashionable German painters. On her orders, for example, in 1779, immediately after the death of Anton Raphael Mengs a large number of works were bought from his studio in Rome. A year later the most celebrated of his paintings in the Hermitage, *Perseus and Andromeda*, arrived from Paris. It has a very interesting story to it. The artist is supposed to have painted it for some Englishman in 1777 and put on display in his Rome studio, where it was received with general delight. The next year the painting was despatched to England by sea, but the ship was seized by French pirates. Mengs's canvas then appeared in Cadiz, where it was sold to the French naval minister, from whom the French encyclopaedist Grimm acquired it for Catherine. Mengs, a leading figure in Neo-Classicism, famed throughout Europe, is represented in the Hermitage with exhaustive completeness. No less popular were his contemporaries Angelika Kauffmann, who produced mainly historical paintings and portraits, and the landscape and battle painter Jacob Phillip Hackert. The Russian Empress commissioned quite a few works from them and other German artists. All this explains why eighteenth-century paintings make up the greater part of the Hermitage collection of German art.

The joint struggle against Napoleon particularly strengthened Russia's ties with Germany. In the nineteenth century many German artists came to Russia to work. Franz Krüger, the favourite portraitist of the Russian court, for example, visited St Petersburg six times and created a whole series of formal likenesses. Two of them — large equestrian portraits of Alexander I and King Frederick William III of Prussia — adorn the 1812 War Gallery in the Winter Palace. During their trips abroad, which invariably included German cities, members of the imperial family visited art exhibitions and studios, actively purchasing paintings.

Much was done for the enlargement of the Hermitage collection by the Romantic poet Vasily Zhukovsky, who held a prominent position at court as tutor to the heir to the throne (the future Alexander II). He took a great interest in art and was personally acquainted with almost all notable German artists. It is to his good taste that the Hermitage owes its splendid collection of the Romantic artist Caspar David Friedrich, rivalled only by that of the Kunsthalle in Hamburg. Zhukovsky, who corresponded with Friedrich, managed to interest Nicholas I (before he came to the throne) in the artist who was without official recognition in his home-land.  In 1820, while in Dresden, Nicholas visited his studio and bought several paintings with which he adorned the "Cottage", his summer palace in Peterhof. Poetic and somewhat melancholy in mood, Friedrich's pictures fitted superbly with the Neo-Gothic architecture of the building and the surrounding landscape park.

In contrast to the French Romantics, German artists of that tendency were not inclined to either civic zeal or sedition. Their best achievements are in the field of landscape painting, but these are landscapes of a particular kind. "A painting should not be invented, but created with feeling," as Friedrich said. The image of nature in the artist's work always reflects his personal, subjective experience, and is constructed on the associations that a particular motif evokes in him.

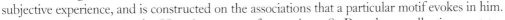

Many paintings in the Hermitage come from private St Petersburg collections put together in the second half of the nineteenth century. The largest among them was the gallery of Count Kushelev-Bezborodko. The most progressive of Russian collectors at that time, he actively acquired works by new European artists, both French and German. In 1862, after the owner's death, the gallery of Count Koshelev-Bezborodko passed under his will to the Academy of Arts, from where it entered the Hermitage in 1922.

Despite its relatively small size, the Hermitage collection of twentieth-century German paintings is now considered one of the best outside Germany. It gives a sufficiently full picture of the main developments over the period and contains works of different genres from the leading artistic centres of the country. One of these was Düsseldorf. The paintings of Düsseldorf artists are marked by a wide variety of subjects, often connected with works of literature, such as the Romantic Karl Friedrich Lessing's large canvas *The Royal Couple Mourning the Death of Their Daughter*.

Besides Dresden and Düsseldorf, there was an active artistic life in Berlin and especially in Munich, which in the late nineteenth century became one of the main European art centres. One of those associated with the city is Franz von Stuck, who ranks among the greatest figures in German art at the turn of the century. A painter, graphic artist, sculptor and architect, he founded the Munich Sezession together with Wilhelm Trübner, and his work is closely linked with the Jugendstil. Stuck's paintings contain echoes of Symbolist poetry. One of the main themes in his work was dark passions, human sinfulness. It this respect the Hermitage's *Fight over a Woman* is typical. Among Stuck's pupils were Kandinsky and Klee, two of the greats of European art in the first half of the twentieth century.

In the first decades of the twentieth century, Germany played an important role in the European avant-garde. Sadly, this part of the Hermitage collection is the least complete and lacks some major artists. Some modern German works came into the Hermitage from Moscow in the 1940s, when the Museum of New Western Art, organized from nationalised private collections, closed. A number of others were donated to the museum by individuals. Most interesting here are the works of Heinrich Campendonk, a participant in the celebrated 1911 *Blauer Reiter* exhibition, organized in Munich by Kandinsky and Klee, and those of the Expressionist Heinrich Ehmsen.

Everything in Cranach's painting suggests his interest in the real world which was so characteristic of the art of the Renaissance, and at the same time shows the artist's knowledge of folk imagery. The golden-haired Mary looking like a princess of an old German fairy-tale, is depicted amidst a beautiful landscape.

Most probably the woman represented in this magnificent painting by the great German master, is not a real sitter, but rather an idealized image — the same type of the face with a small pointed chin and almond-shaped eyes can be met in Cranach's other paintings, such as The Virgin and Child under the Apple-Tree.

AMBROSIUS HOLBEIN (CA. 1495 – CA. 1520)
Portrait of a Young Man
1518

Basle, to which the young Holbein brothers arrived from their native Augsburg,
was in the early sixteenth century one of major centres of Humanism in Germany and
had close ties with Italy. It was not a mere coincidence that the type of portrait in
an architectural setting characteristic of the Italian Renaissance was popular there.
However, the ultimate concreteness in the rendering of human appearance and
a "Northern melancholy" lend a distinctly German character to the works of Holbein.

Mengs always drew inspiration for his own work from classical examples. The figure of Perseus, for instance, bears an apparent resemblance to the celebrated statue of Apollo the Belvedere, while Andromeda is modelled on an ancient Roman relief. The concept of the painting was inspired by the ancient cameo which was owned by his wife and now is in the Hermitage collection.

CASPAR DAVID FRIEDRICH (1774–1840)
On a SailingShip
1818–19

The ship sailing on the sea is one of the most favourite images in Romantic poetry. Depicted in the foreground of the picture, it seems to be driven forward not so much by the power of wind as by the feelings of the two people whose glances are attracted to the distant and unknown shores. It is known that this work was painted by Friedrich shortly after his honeymoon trip to the north of Germany. The heroes of the painting are usually identified as the romanticized self-portrait of the artist with his wife Caroline, and the picture as a whole is interpreted in the allegoric sense of their mutual journey over the "sea of life", their mutual aspiration towards noble aims.

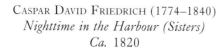

CASPAR DAVID FRIEDRICH (1774–1840)
Nighttime in the Harbour (Sisters)
Ca. 1820

People are often present in Friedrich's landscapes. Shown with their backs to the viewers, they seem to be steeped in a silent contemplation of distant views — like the women standing on the shore of a harbour at night who are watching sailing ships and probably dreaming of remote countries. Soaring amidst the masts are twin Gothic towers, a motif which is characteristic of German Romantic painters who were fascinated with the Middle Ages.

CARL FRIEDRICH LESSING (1808–1880)
The Royal Couple Mourning the Death of Their Daughter
1830

This is the first large-scale painting by this Düsseldorf Romantic which was displayed at the 1830 exhibition in Berlin and won general acclaim. Many researchers believed that its subject is based on the ballad The Castle on the Water *by the Romantic poet Uhland, yet Lessing himself asserted that he had never read this poem and painted it under the impression of the death of a young girl who was very popular in Düsseldorf society. The real event has been transformed by the artist into an image of the distant Middle Ages, a device which was characteristic of Romantic art.*

FRANZ VON STUCK (1863–1928)
Fight over a Woman
1905

The theme of the picture was inspired by works of Friedrich
Nietzsche which exerted a marked influence on European art
of the turn of the century. This theme was one of the main subjects
of Stuck's work. He devoted to this subject twenty-five works
painted in different periods. Showing the power of man's carnal
instincts, the artist deliberately emphasizes the brutality of
the figures which seem to be brought out from the dark background
by an uneven light, the bright flashes of which contrast sharply
with the dull shadows.

A *participant of the celebrated Blauer Reiter exhibition organized by Wassily Kandinsky in Munich in 1911, as well as of other exhibitions during that period, Campedonk was mobilized at the beginning of the First World War. The war events became a great shock for the artist. In the late 1910s he led an isolated life in a village wholly plunging into the realm of idyllic images in which he sought a salvation from cruel reality. Campedonck's painting* Man and Animals Amidst Nature *built on the juxtaposition of coloured planes is characteristic of the artist, who was fascinated with old stained windows.*

HEINRICH EHMSEN
(1886–1964)
*The Shooting
(The Red Jacket)*
1919

T*his Expressionist painting, remarkable for its distorted figures and sharp colour contrasts, was executed under the impression of a real event witnessed by the artist — the bloody murder of the leaders of the Bavarian Republic in 1919. "They shot the revolutionaries in the courtyard of the barracks," Ehmsen recollected. "I felt as a possessed one trying to convey my anger in drawings and paintings."*

English
Painting *16th to 19th Century*

The Hermitage's collection of English painting is not large. In the eighteenth century, when it began, Russia was virtually the only country in Europe that took a serious interest in English art. The Walpole collection acquired by Catherine the Great included works by English paint-ers whose names then meant little to collectors or connoisseurs. Still, they laid the foundation for a collection that by the end of the century included paintings by famous English artists, often bought directly from them. That was the case in 1774 with *An Iron Forge* by Joseph Wright of Derby, a painting that had enjoyed great success at home. A little later two further large landscapes by that original and distinctive talent appeared in the Winter Palace.

In December 1785 Joshua Reynolds — the most influential English artist, first president of the Royal Academy, venerated in his homeland as a great portraitist and outstanding theoretician — received a flattering commission from the Russian court to paint two large pictures on a historical subject. One painting was intended for Empress Catherine the Great, the other for Prince Potemkin. For Catherine the Great Reynolds chose a subject from ancient mythology, the infant Hercules killing two monstrous snakes in his cradle. The scene was an allegory glorifying the power and might of the young Russian Empire. For Prince Potemkin the subject was taken from Roman history — *The Forbearance of Scipio Africanus*, alluding to the virtue of the Empress's all-powerful favourite. Prince Potemkin also commissioned Reynolds to make a replica of one of his best known works, the brilliant *Venus and Cupid*.

Reynolds worked enthusiastically on the two enormous canvases over two years. Finally, in 1789, the pair, held to be the ageing master's best works, were despatched. Catherine was very pleased with her acquisition which was installed in one of the halls of the Winter Palace, but the artist never saw his fee. The 1,500 guineas were paid to Reynolds's heirs only after repeated reminders. In 1792, after Potemkin's death, the Hermitage acquired two other works by the artist from the Prince's collection.

Thus, by the nineteenth century, a wholly representative collection of English painting, probably one of the best outside England, had formed in the Hermitage. As the century advanced, English paintings were acquired for the Hermitage and suburban imperial residences, and also by numerous private collectors. Moreover, individual English painters drawn by the wealth and generosity of the Russian aristocracy, began arriving in the capital in search of profitable commissions.

The career of the portraitist George Dawe is closely connected to St Petersburg and the Winter Palace. In the autumn of 1818 members of the Congress of Vienna, leaders of the coalition against Napoleon Bonaparte, met in Aachen. Naturally this event, attended by European monarchs and their high-ranking retinues, attracted many artists hoping for well-paid work. The little known Englishman George Dawe obtained a commission for a portrait of Russian General Bagration. Dawe's speed of working and ability to capture a likeness attracted the attention of Alexander I, who invited the artist to St Petersburg to work on portraits of the generals who fought in the War of 1812, intended for the commemorative gallery in the Winter Palace. In the ten years he spent in Russia, from 1819 to 1829, Dawe managed to paint hundreds of portraits. Besides the 332 works still in the 1812 War Gallery, he was inundated with commissions from the St Petersburg aristocracy, delighted with the virtuoso skill that could create a portrait in only a few hours of sitting.

Between the 1830s and 1850s the salon portraitist Christina Robertson, a typical exponent of the "official Victorian" style, worked in the Russian capital. Commissioned portraits of the Victorian era were marked by sentimentality, idealization and a love of carefully conveying the texture of fabrics and accessories. In the Hermitage collection her striking, but somewhat superficial talent is well demonstrated by a portrait of Nicholas I's daughters.

For all the acquisitions, up until the early twentieth century the English collection looked quite fragmentary. In 1912 the Hermitage received a generous bequest in the form of Alexei Khitrovo's collection of English paintings. It provided remarkable works by outstanding eight-

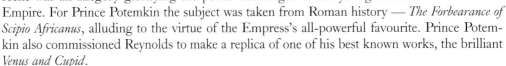

eenth- and early-nineteenth-century artists: Gainsborough, Romney, Hoppner, Raeburn, Opie and Lawrence. After 1917 the Hermitage acquired a fair number of English paintings from private collections and also from the suburban imperial residences.

The greater part of the paintings in the halls of English art are portraits. From its six-teenth-century beginnings to the early nineteenth century, the portrait was the leading genre in English art. England experienced its Renaissance fairly late, in the second half of the sixteenth century, but it did not produce a painting genius on a par with Shakespeare or Francis Bacon. Painting did not occupy a leading place in English culture. An early milestone was Hans Holbein's coming to London at the invitation of Henry VIII. The great German portraitist lived more than ten years in England and his works became a true, if unattainable school of craftsmanship for his English contemporaries and followers. At that time there were hardly any "home-grown" English artists; painters came  to the country from the Low Countries and Germany. The Hermitage's portraits of the late sixteenth and early seventeenth centuries, a tremendous rarity outside England, are attributed to Hans Eworth and Marcus Gheeraerts the Younger, both from the Low Countries.

The next notable event in English artistic life was the arrival in the 1620s, at the invitation of Charles I, of the great Flemish portraitist Anthony van Dyck, who lived in London until his death in 1641. The English consider him the founder of their national school. It was Van Dyck who managed to raise the fairly low prestige of the artist to unprecedented heights. By the end of the seventeenth century, English painting was approaching its heyday, which is associated with three outstanding masters — William Hogarth, Joshua Reynolds and Thomas Gains-borough. Sadly, there are no works by Hogarth in the Hermitage, while Reynolds, who was celebrated chiefly for his portraits, is represented, as has been said, by historical genre pieces which he painted quite rarely.

Among the indubitable masterpieces of English painting is the *Portrait of a Lady in Blue* by Gainsborough, one of the eighteenth century's most original and poetic artists. He, probably more than other English painters, can be regarded as the spiritual heir to Van Dyck. His painting is striking for the wealth of shades and virtuoso technique, yet at the same time Gainsborough's models display a special refinement, a spirituality of feelings, qualities present in full measure in the artist himself. Painted in a delicate palette of pale blues and silvers, the *Lady in Blue* dates from the 1770s, when Gainsborough's talent was at its height.

The glorious portrait tradition was continued at the beginning of the next century by Thomas Lawrence. His talent was known far beyond Britain and the crowned heads, diplo-mats and generals of Europe considered it an honour to pose for this president of the Royal Academy and painter to the king. The Hermitage's portraits of members of the Vorontsov family allow us to judge this outstanding artist.

At the turn of the nineteenth century English painting began to influence European art, particularly French. Delacroix and Géricault admired Lawrence's portraits. This period also saw the stunning rise of English landscape painting. Discoveries made by Turner and Constable (alas, not represented in the Hermitage) shaped the development of the genre in Europe for the best part of the century. Two Hermitage paintings by Richard Parkes Bonington, one of the favourite artists of the French innovators, form a sort of bridge to the continent. In the second half of the nineteenth century, English art reached another highpoint with the work of the Pre-Raphaelite Brotherhood, but sadly they too are absent from the Hermitage.

Marcus Gheeraerts studied painting under his father, an artist who came to England from the Netherlands. Towards the seventeenth century he grew into a leading English painter and was granted the title of court painter. His painting is marked by a certain dryness and dark colour scheme, yet his portraits faithfully recreate the characters of the eventful reign of Queen Elizabeth.

JOSHUA REYNOLDS (1723–1792)
Cupid Untying the Girdle
of Venus
1788

_T*his inspired painting is a brilliant example of Reynolds's gift as a colourist. The radiant combinations of reds, yellows and blues recall that the artist's favourite painters were Venetian masters of the sixteenth century. Venus painted by Reynolds is far from the ideal of classical beauty — her image is based on a representation of a smart red-haired English model.*

THOMAS GAINSBOROUGH
(1727–1788)
Portrait of a Lady in Blue
Late 1770s

On entering the Hermitage collection this masterpiece by Gainsborough was listed as a portrait of the Duchess de Beaufort, the wife of the French ambassador to the English court. However, there is no evidence that Gainsborough painted anybody from the duke's family. Beautiful to this day as a romantic dream, the stranger still remains a mysterious "lady in blue".

GEORGE MORLAND
(1763–1804)
Approaching Storm
1791

During his short life
Morland produced about four
hundred paintings the major
part of which are landscapes
and genre scenes. Born into the
family of hereditary artists and
married to the daughter of the
well-known engraver Ward,
Morland, however, preferred
not to spend time in drawing
rooms of high society, but to
lead a dissolute life of a
bohemian among fellow
artists, jockeys and gamblers.
He spent the last years of his
life in a debtor's prison and
was set free shortly before his
death. The Approaching
Storm *is considered to be one
of Morland's best paintings
notable for immediacy and
somewhat naïve realism.*

JOSEPH WRIGHT OF DERBY
(1743–1797)
*An Iron Forge Viewed
from Without*
1773

Joseph Wright was the first
English painter who turned
to the subjects illustrating the
mysterious world of scientific
discoveries and interesting
natural phenomena. The circle
of his friends consisted of scholars,
philosophers, industrialists and
inventors. The eminent Russian
artist and art critic Alexander
Benois wrote about An Iron
Forge: "This painting serves
as a fine example of Wright's
technical perfection. It shows
a slice of life as it was seen by
the artist in all its ingenuity."

THOMAS LAWRENCE (1769–1830)
Portrait of Count Mikhail Vorontsov
1821

C*ount Mikhail Vorontsov, from 1853 His Excellency Prince, was a prominent
Russian statesman and military figure. He spent his childhood and youth in England
where his father, Count Sergei Vorontsov, was the Russian ambassador for more than
forty years. The young count, having received a brilliant education in England, returned
to Russia in 1801 to enter the military service. He took part in the 1812 War against
Napoleon and was wounded near Borodino. In 1819, on coming to London for a visit
to his father, he commissioned his portrait to Lawrence, the most fashionable English
painter of this period. The portrait of the count, who is represented in the uniform
of the general, with the three stars of the Russian orders, features the romantic image
of a victor and hero.*

GEORGE DAWE (1781–1829)
Portrait of General Piotr Bagration
1823

Portrait of Prince Piotr Bagration ranks among the best works by Dawe created for the 1812 War Gallery in the Winter Palace. The glory of Bagration, the descendant of Georgian princes, who had been known for his incomparable bravery from Suvorov's Italian and Swiss campaigns, spread wide beyond the borders of Russia. In 1812 the general died of wounds during the Battle of Borodino and therefore Dawe had to paint the portrait from representations made during Bagration's lifetime.

CHRISTINA ROBERTSON (1775–1856)
Children with a Parrot
1850s

Commissioned portraits by Christina Robertson, who was elected a member of the St Petersburg Academy of Arts, were notable for their sentimentality and Salon-style prettiness. But her virtuoso rendering of the texture of fabrics and idealization of outward features of high-rank sitters made the paintress a desirable guest in high society at St Petersburg, Vienna and Berlin. The portraits she created in different countries show little variety — they feature equally stately men, lovely women and charming children, and only their minor details allow one to surmise where they could be painted. An Orthodox church in the background of this portrait suggests that it was produced in Russia.

french

Painting *16th to 20th Century*

umerous masterpieces adorn the collection of French art that is justly considered the pride of the Hermitage. It fills more than fifty rooms in the Winter Palace and represents almost all styles and tendencies in French art, and almost all the country's leading artists. Outside of France no other collection can compare for quantity and quality. Many of the seventeenth- and eighteenth-century masterpieces were acquired by Catherine the Great who was noted for her love of French style and fashion. Among the connoisseurs and professionals who advised Catherine on questions of art were the noted French encyclopaedists Diderot and Grimm. It was due to them that the collection came to include works by Poussin, Lorrain, Le Nain and other great seventeenth-century artists. Diderot kept his patroness constantly informed about developments in the Paris art world. He was instrumental in the acquisition of the most famous works by contemporary artists recognized at official exhibitions.

In the eighteenth century the French collection grew richer in several ways: by the acquisition of whole private collections, the purchase of individual masterpieces, and commissions to living artists.

The Gotzkowsky collection, which laid the foundation of the Hermitage gallery, included, among mainly Dutch and Flemish works, French eighteenth-century paintings. Count Brühl's collection brought two Watteau masterpieces in 1768. Some superb examples of French painting graced Walpole's collection, which came to the Hermitage at the end of the century. In 1772, though, the Empress acquired the collection without which the museum's French stocks would not be what it is. Its founder, Pierre de Crozat, one of the richest men in France, invested the greater part of his fortune in works of art, creating one of the finest collections in Europe. After his death the paintings, graphic art and engraved gemstones passed to his nephew who sold them to Catherine. This superb collection contained about 500 paintings by great artists of various schools; French art was represented by Poussin, Watteau, Lancret and Chardin masterpieces.

In the late eighteenth century, many private collections, belonging to the St Petersburg aristocracy, began to appear. Many of them, evolving with time, survived into the twentieth century and after the 1917 revolution added to the Hermitage's collection of French painting.

Private collections were shaped by the tastes of the owners, which did not always coincide with those of the experts. Often Russian nobles were in close contact with artists, buying works at auction or straight from the studio.

Count Alexander Stroganov sharply criticized contemporary French painting for lack of great ideas, but enjoyed the work of the landscape artists Vernet and Robert, and was on good personal terms with Greuze. These artists were particularly popular with Russian collectors in the late eighteenth century, including Emperor Paul I. Prince Nikolai Yusupov was friendly with the then-fashionable portraitist Elisabeth Vigée-Lebrun and corresponded with Fragonard and Greuze. It is to such personal ties that the Hermitage owes its extensive collection of late Rococo works.

From the start of the nineteenth century, the Hermitage's French collection almost stopped receiving new works. The stormy age of the French Revolution and Napoleonic Wars afforded artists no opportunity of getting their works into Russia's imperial museum. The isolated works by artists who regenerated French art and made France a centre of world culture, which reached Russia together with a host of second-rate works by salon artists of the day, were acquired by noted St Petersburg collectors — Count Kushelev-Bezborodko, the Duke of Leuchtenberg, the Yusupov, Sheremetyev and Naryshkin families. Their collections, mostly nationalized after 1917, formed the main stock of French art from the first half of the nineteenth century. The largest St Petersburg collection of contemporary European — to a considerable extent French — painting belonged to Count Nikolai Kushelev-Bezborodko (1834–1862) who spent his enormous inheritance on pictures. Incurably ill, a few years before his death (in Nice at the age of 28), the Count began to attend all major exhibitions of contemporary art in Europe and created the collection that he bequeathed to the St Petersburg Academy of Arts. In 1922 it was transferred to the Hermitage.

The majority of the works collected by the Count were by fashionable painters of the day, celebrated artists of the Paris Salon, which in the first half of the nineteenth century was the only official exhibition venue where artists could seek clients, fame and commercial success. The names of many Salon celebrities are now known only to experts, and they account for the greater part of the Hermitage collection for this period, although through Kushelev-Bezborodko the museum also acquired works by artists of enduring fame — Delacroix, Théodore Rousseau, Jules Dupré, Daubigny, Corot, Courbet and Millet.

The world-famous Hermitage collection of French art from the second half of the nineteenth century and the beginning of the twentieth comes mainly from the collections of two outstanding Moscow-based collectors, Sergei Shchukin and Ivan Morozov. Successful businessmen and heirs to large fortunes, they also possessed fine artistic taste, daring and that special sixth sense that enabled them in a brief space of time to assemble unique collections of the latest French art. At the time it did indeed require a special audacity to buy Impressionist paintings that were considered crude daubs by the general public in Russia.

Even more intrepid independence was needed to buy works by the little known members of the Parisian avant-garde, Matisse and Picasso. Often guided only by their own intuition, the Russian collectors bought

frighteningly innovative paintings that were only acknowledged as masterpieces decades later. The Moscow mansions of Shchukin and Morozov, packed with the best works of the French avant-garde, became places of pilgrimage for young Russian artists, acting as a school of modern art. After the revolution Shchukin's gallery became the First Museum of New Western Art, Morozov's the Second. In 1928 the two museums were combined. In the early 1930s, following the Old Masters from the Hermitage, its best works began to be sold out of the country. Cézanne's *Pierrot and Harlequin* and Van Gogh's *Night Café* ended up in private collections abroad. In 1948, at the height of the repressions and the struggle against "cosmopolitanism and veneration of the West", the museum was closed. According to the order signed by Stalin, some works were to be destroyed, and the best transferred to the Hermitage and the Pushkin Museum of Fine Arts. On the whole, the works of French artists were divided roughly equally. The Pushkin Museum was more interested in Impressionists and Post-Impressionists, therefore the Hermitage collection is slightly inferior to the Moscow one in that respect, but the Hermitage acquired a number of excellent works by Picasso, Matisse and Derain, as well as unique monumental canvases by Denis and Bonnard.

The "ideologically dangerous" works were, however, condemned to a long stay in the Hermitage storerooms, forbidden to be viewed even by experts. Only after Stalin's death in the middle of the 1950s did the Impressionists and Post-Impressionists gradually appear in the museum halls, followed in the 1960s by Matisse and Picasso. This at last made it possible to trace the whole development of French art, from the Middle Ages to the twentieth century.

Compared to the very rich seventeenth-century stocks, the Renaissance, which began late in France, in the second half of the sixteenth century, is hardly represented. Collectors only began to show interest in this important stage in the development of French art, long overshadowed by the Italian and Netherlandish Renaissance and later French art, when the Hermitage painting collection was in the main complete. There is, however, a small, but tastefully selected collection of portraits (including a small masterpiece by Pierre Dumoustier) that to some extent allows us to form a true picture of refined French Renaissance culture, in which aristocratic convention combined with a love of the individual and characteristic.

The seventeenth century saw the beginning of the triumph of French art. The great artist of the age Nicolas Poussin — head of the austere, elevated system of French Classicism — is represented in the Hermitage by twelve works. Twelve majestically beautiful Classical landscapes by Claude Lorrain and genre pieces by Louis Le Nain elaborate on the style created by Poussin that determined the main qualities of French seventeenth-century art.

Antoine Watteau was at the source of the style that shaped French eighteenth-century art, the playfully skilful Rococo. The Hermitage can boast eight masterpieces by Watteau. Striking skill and an easy freedom are demonstrated by the best artists of the Rococo, François  Boucher and Jean-Honoré Fragonard, who are represented in the Hermitage collection by various facets of their rich artistic legacy. The Hermitage's three paintings by Jean-Baptiste-Siméon Chardin brilliantly show the ability of this great master of the second half of the eighteenth century to find in modest, everyday subjects the spirituality, harmony and poetry present in the works of his great predecessors, Poussin, Le Nain and Watteau.

The remarkable collection of nineteenth- and early-twentieth-century French painting housed on the second floor reflects all the complex, at times dramatic struggle of different tendencies, changes of styles and leaders, that characterised the art of this period. The first direction, born back on the eve of the 1789 revolution, Neo-Classicism, Romanticism that replaced it in the 1820s, and Realism that came a decade later are all represented by both the works of leading artists and numerous pieces by their followers and rivals, the popular representatives of the official art of the Salon.

The Hermitage collection of works from the following periods is justly considered one of the best in the world. Paintings by Monet, Renoir, Degas, Pissarro and Sisley reflect the distinctive quality of the Impressionists' method, based on working directly from nature.

Cézanne, Van Gogh and Gauguin, for all their apparent diversity of tastes, passions, origins and education, had much in common. As lone rebels they pushed off from Impressionism to discover their own methods of interpreting reality in painting. They are therefore known as the Post-Impressionists. Paul Cézanne dreamt of making Impressionism "eternal, solid, like the art in museums". The painting of the tormented Dutchman Vincent van Gogh, is also to a large extent founded on Impressionist achievements, but his colours are determined not by nature, but by the emotions that possessed him as he worked. The Hermitage's four Van Goghs were painted in the final, most dramatic period of his life.

Together with Cézanne and Van Gogh at the root of twentieth-century art was Paul Gauguin. The Hermitage has fifteen of his works, dating from his period on Tahiti. He found on the distant South Sea island a paradise, a "Golden Age" in which he hoped to rediscover what European civilization had lost — the feeling of harmony and balance needed to create perfect works of art.

The painting of the Nabis group (Hebrew for "prophets") combines in a way the classical traditions, the main achievements of the nineteenth century with the dawning age of revolutionary discoveries. In 1905 Matisse and his friends earned themselves the nickname *Fauves* ("wild beasts"), while two years later Picasso hit upon Cubism. A final crescendo is sounded in the French collection by the works of those two twentieth-century tendencies.

The biographical data on
*Pierre Dumoustier, an eminent
master of the French Renaissance, is rather scant. It is known
that he came from a large
family of artists. Pierre and
his elder brother Etienne won
fame as talented portraitists.
They achieved great results in
the medium of pencil portraiture which was particularly
popular in France during the last
decades of the sixteenth century.
Pierre Dumoustier was active
at the court of Queen Catherine
de' Medici in Paris. The manner
of painting in this* Portrait
of a Youth *is almost as transparent as that of a watercolour.
The canvas is Dumoustier's
only oil painting which has
reached us. The image of a young
intellectual engrossed with his
profound thoughts and feelings,
gives an idea of the French
character formed under the
influence of Humanist ideas
of the Renaissance.*

This painting is a masterpiece by the celebrated Louis Le Nain, an artist who belonged to the circle of the so-called "painters of the real world". The subject matter of the canvas, an example of the "peasant genre", is devoid of any narrative or entertaining details. The peasant family, with a donkey and dog looking like its members, depicted against the huge greyish-blue sky, evokes a feeling of dignity and self-reliance. The characteristically French love for a balanced and thought-out composition enhances a lofty universal meaning of the scene.

Nicolas Poussin (1594–1665)
Venus, Faun and Putt
1630s

Poussin, a devoted exponent of harmony and perfection of classical art, regarded the ancient Greek civilization as the Golden Age of mankind. Living in Italy, he worked out his austere classicist doctrine based on a profound study of ancient monuments and works by great masters of the Renaissance. Even the very air of Italy, its beauty, as he believed, was a necessary condition for the creation of lofty and noble art of Classicism. The theme of bacchanals, ancient festivals dedicated to the god of wine Bacchus, interested Poussin who devoted to it a number of his works in the so-called Venetian cycle pervaded with a truly pagan joy of life.
The picture Venus, Faun and Putti was evidently one of numerous studies in which the artist developed this theme.

NICOLAS POUSSIN (1594–1665)
Tancred and Erminia
1630s

The great Poussin declared that the picture begins with
a subjet which must have a noble character. His Tancred and
Erminia *is based on the poem* Jerusalem Delivered *by
Torquato Tasso, the Italian poet of the Renaissance. The scene
chosen by the artist deals with the love of a pagan woman,
Erminia, who knew the secrets of magic, to a noble knight, the
crusader Tancred. The knight, eager to make heroic feats for his
holy faith, set out for the Crusade. On learning that Tancred was
mortally wounded in a battle with the giant Organt, Erminia
discovered the dying knight on the battlefield and saved him.
She cut off her hair which possessed magic power to bind his
wounds, but on doing this for the sake of love, Erminia lost her
magic gift for ever.*

NICOLAS POUSSIN (1594–1665)
Landscape with Polythemus
1649

In the late 1640s Poussin created a series of majestic and splendid landscapes devoted to the harmonious unity of eternal Nature and all the creatures inhabiting it. The earth, trees, mountains, gods, people, nymphs and satyrs seem to listen, holding their breath, to the magic sounds of a pipe played by the cyclop Polyphemus who, seated on a rock, is pouring out his sad feelings connected with his unrequited love to the beautiful sea-nymph Galatea.

CLAUDE LORRAIN (CLAUDE GELLÉ) (1600–1682)
Morning in a Harbour
1640s

Paintings by Lorrain who came to Italy as a youth and spent his whole life there, served as a standard of an elevated classical landscape for many generations of French painters. No less thoroughly composed than paintings by Poussin, they are filled with a profound lyrical feeling of the artist and his delight at the beautiful scenery of Campagna. The special light effects characteristic of the Italian countryside in varying conditions at different times of day are captured by Lorrain in all their subtlety.

ANTOINE WATTEAU (1684–1721)
Embarrassing Proposal
Ca. 1617

Th*is painting belongs to the so-called* fêtes galantes*, a kind of festive scenes introduced by Watteau and recalling a theatrical performance devoted to the theme of love with actors skilfully playing their roles. The scene, almost entirely devoid of outward action, is pervaded with profound emotional undertones. The young girls and cavaliers in gaily coloured garments with streaming folds seem to be separated from the world of the viewer by a transparent wall; their fragile, exquisite, a little sorrowful world is inaccessible as a beautiful dream.*

ANTOINE WATTEAU (1684–1721)
La Capricieuse
Ca. 1718

Th*e* Capricious Girl *is recognized as one of Watteau's masterpieces. The gallant scene of a "siege" undertaken by a cavalier experienced in the game of love for the seduction of a young beauty, charming, proud and capricious, is transformed by Watteau into a pageant of colour and light, delightful for its subtlest shades and half-tones. It seems that life was too crude for the artist and in each new work he created a strikingly poetic and imaginative world of dreams. The great Watteau died of tuberculosis at the age of thirty-seven.*

FRANÇOIS BOUCHER (1703–1770)
Landscape in the Environs of Bauvais
Early 1740s

Paintings by Boucher perhaps most fully epitomize the festive and lively spirit of the mature Rococo. With an equal dexterity he rendered an exquisite pastoral scene, a landscape or a portrait, and he had no problems with designing a stage set, a costume, a tapestry or a porcelain piece. The most fashionable artist of his time, he had the title of the first painter to the King. He was also President of the Academy of Arts and the director of the Royal Tapestry Factory. Boucher worked for the tapestry factory at Beauvais since 1734. This Landscape in the Environs of Beauvais does not feature any real scene — an ornate decorative picture, it would beautifully match an interior fashioned in the Rococo style.

The great master of the Age of the Enlightenment, Chardin was, according to a unanimous opinion of his contemporaries, an inventor of a "rare and special genre" — with great love and warmth he painted small intimate scenes from the daily life of modest representatives of the third estate. The artist himself grew up in this milieu, and his portrayals of the unhurried, measured tenor of life, revealing simple human virtues, are ultimately sincere and benevolent. Moreover, the artist brush has an amazing capacity for investing a most common everyday scene with a sense of poetry and harmony reminiscent of painted masterpieces by his great predecessors Nicolas Poussin, Louis Le Nain and Antoine Watteau.

JEAN-BAPTISTE SIMÉON CHARDIN
(1699–1779)
Laundress
Late 1730s

Not inferior in the finesse of his colour scheme even to Watteau himself, Chardin conveys the texture of objects, their volumes and lighting with a great mastery. The artist applies paint on to the canvas in small but very dense, divided strokes reminiscent of mosaics. At a short range this technique looks almost Impressionistic, but at a distance it strikes one by its illusion of volume, palpability of details and wealth of shades of colour and light.

JEAN-BAPTISTE SIMÉON CHARDIN (1699–1779)
Still Life with the Attributes of Arts
1766

Chardin *began his career as a painter from still lifes and devoted to this kind of painting, which was then considered the lowest form of art, his entire rare talent. This still-life painting dealing with the subject of the arts was created specially for the St Petersburg Academy of Arts during the later part of Chardin's lifetime. The objects depicted in the painting are endowed with a feeling of dignity and noble restraint, unobtrusively suggesting to the viewer their symbolic message — the books on the table symbolize the history of art, the brushes and paints refer to painting, the drawings with a plan of the eastern colonnade of the Louvre created by Charles Perrault denote architecture, the ancient vessels allude to archaeology, the statue* Mercury Tying His Sandals *by Jean-Baptiste Pigalle implies sculpture and the Order of the Legion of Honour lying in the foreground is a reminder that the efforts of artists can be rewarded by the highest decoration of France.*

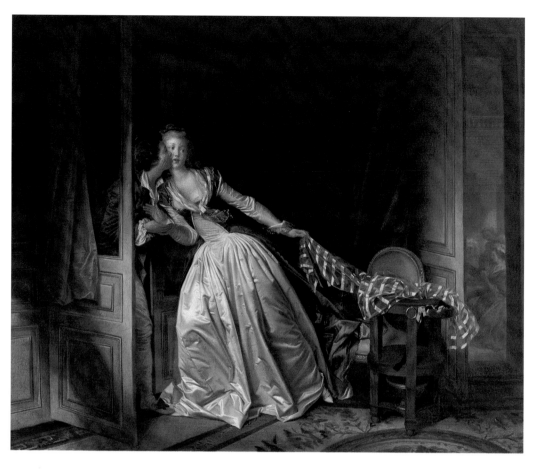

Fragonard is at his best in conveying the sincere joy of living. An outright improviser, he was a brilliant master enjoying general renown, "Frago", as he was affectionately called. His canvases, which were admired by his contemporaries for his unrivalled skill in capturing transient feelings, have never lost their attraction to viewers thanks to their vivid spontaneity. The artist had an equally free command of different artistic techniques. For its loving attention to detail and faithful rendering of the texture of materials, Fragonard's Snatched Kiss recalls paintings by the Small Dutch Masters.

JEAN-BAPTISTE GREUZE (1725–1805)
Portrait of Count Pavel Stroganov as a Child
1778

Count Pavel A. Stroganov (1772–1817) was the son of Count Alexander S. Stroganov, an eminent dignitary in the age of Catherine the Great, President of the Academy of Arts. In his youth Pavel Stroganov took part in the French Revolution and during the reign of Alexander I he was a notable diplomat. He was a hero of the 1812 War against Napoleon Bonaparte. The portrait was painted by Greuze in Paris when the Stroganov family stayed there and when the boy was six years old.

JEAN-BAPTISTE PERRONNEAU (1715–1783)
Portrait of a Boy with a Book
1740s

The brilliant portraitist of the Rococo era, Peronneau was active in Paris, London and Amsterdam, and there is a supposition that in 1781 he visited St Petersburg. His favourite technique was pastel in which he attained perfect results. The glory of his outstanding contemporaries, La Tour, Chardin and Fragonard, eclipsed the more lyrical gift of Perronneau, but his Portrait of a Boy with a Book *painted in oils is not inferior to works by the more famous masters either in the virtuoso manner of painting or in the depth of psychological penetration.*

ANTOINE JEAN GROS (1771–1835)
Napoleon Bonaparte on the Bridge
at Arcole
Replica of the 1797 painting

Gros, the favourite pupil of Jacques Louis David, the head of the Neo-Classical School, depicts a moment of triumph of General Napoleon Bonaparte, the young commander of the French army, during the battle against the Austrians at Arcole in Italy (15–17 November 1796).

FRANÇOIS GÉRARD (1770–1837)
Portrait of Joséphine de Beuharnais
1801

The well-known portrait painter Gérard, also a pupil of David, painted Joséphine, Napoleon's first wife, on the terrace of her Malmaison Palace near Paris. This was then a new, Neo-Classical type of formal portraiture, intently devoid of luxury and abundant accessories typical of commissioned portraits popular in the previous period. Joséphine, a passionate Creole woman, wears, in keeping with the fashion of the age, a simple white dress that does not conceal the shapes of her body.

JACQUES LOUIS DAVID (1748–1825)
Sappho and Phaon
1809

This painting was commissioned from the celebrated creator of Neo-Classicism by Prince Nikolai
Yusupov. The image of Sappho, a famous ancient Greek poetess, attracted many Neo-Classical
artists. Already not young, she fell in love with the young Phaon and took a suicide unable to suffer
the pains of unrequited love. Everything in the picture is sustained in the spirit of classical
examples — from the subject and clothes of the heroes to the details of furniture and garments
which David modelled, after a thorough study, on works of ancient art.

LOUIS LÉOPOLD BOILLY
(1761–1845)
Billiards. 1807

This painting was acquired by Nikolai Yusupov in Paris. The best of the nine Hermitage canvases by Boilly, a well-known master of the genre in the Hermitage collection, it shows elegant women in tight-fitting dresses who are playing the game of billiards. This subject, impossible during the earlier period, indicates the radical changes which took place in society after the revolution. A billiards room became a sort of club where people gathered not only to play but to exchange news, to make acquaintances and to flirt.

HORACE VERNET (1789–1863)
Self-Portrait
1835

Horace Vernet was born into a well-known French artistic family. His grandfather Claude Joseph Vernet was a noted eighteenth-century landscape painter. Horace Vernet was idolized by visitors to the mid-nineteenth-century Salons in Paris. His paintings, romantic in spirit yet marked by a careful finish, enraptured the public. This self-portrait is based on Oriental motifs which were so popular among the Romantic artists. The artist depicted himself in an austere setting of his Roman studio, wearing an Oriental costume and smoking a hookah, amidst valuable objects brought from the East, such as a carpet, a dagger and a pistol.

EUGÈNE DELACROIX (1798–1863)
Arab Saddling His Horse
1855

The great Delacroix treated Oriental motifs with all the passion of his unbridled Romantic temperament.
The artist made a travel to Algeria and Morocco as early as 1832, but twenty years later his Moroccan impressions
sounded as a spontaneous and powerful chord in his paintings. A seemingly ordinary occurrence, captured by the artist's
swift brush, is pervaded with energy and dynamism. In a few minutes the fleeting scene, which evokes a sense
of inner unity of the man and the horse, will disappear.

JEAN LÉON GERÔME
(1824–1904)
The Sale of a Slave
1884

The most notable representative of the Salon, Gerôme was granted nearly all kinds of official honours, titles and awards which a French artist could dream of — medals of the Salon, the Légion d'Honneur, the title of Academician, etc. The Sale of a Slave *had a tremendous success in the Salon of 1884 where it was displayed as* The Sale of Slaves in Rome. *However, the artist's contemporaries were not unanimous in their admiration of his mastery. Emile Zola, for example, wrote in an article addressing to the artist: "You have a perfect command of your craft, your fingers are amazingly skilful. Yet your talent is that of a worker. I am in vain looking for a creator. You have neither inspiration nor character, nor any individuality."*

FRANÇOIS XAVIER WINTERHALTER (1806–1873)
Portrait of Countess Sophia Naryshkina
1858

This portrait of Countess Sophia Naryshkina, the wife of the Chamberlain Kirill Naryshkin, belongs to the hand of the popular Salon portrait painter and was produced in the mid-nineteenth century in Paris. Winterhalter was famous for his ability to paint very rapidly and skilfully, focusing on the sheen of fabrics, the glitter of gems and the softness of furs, which embellished his aristocratic customers. Members of the upper crust of St Petersburg society dreamed of his portraits, and that is why about fifteen portraits executed by this master are in the Hermitage collection.

THÉODORE ROUSSEAU (1812–1867)
Marketplace in Normandy
1832

It is to Rousseau that French art lovers owed the discovery of the beautiful national scenery which had previously been pushed into the background by the garish magnificence of Italian views. In order to completely plunge into a study of his native countryside, Rousseau left Paris and settled in the village of Barbizon where he was soon followed by his friends and like-minded artists. Thus the famous Barbizon school which evolved a new kind of French landscape came into being. The Barbizons laid the emphasis in landscape painting on a direct study from nature. The Market in Normandy does not look like a thought-out picture painted in a studio, but like an immediate study permeated with the living pulsation of a real scene.

Troyon, *a well-known Salon painter, took an interest in the work of the Barbizon artists and frequently joined them on painting tours in the picturesque environs of their favourite Forest of Fontainebleau. His large-scale paintings featuring herds of cows and sheep wandering along roads or grazing around Barbizon enjoyed a great success with art lovers.*

The "magician Corot", as he was sometimes called by his contemporaries, painted his landscapes permeated with light and filled with a poetic sense of nature as if he had "wings behind his back". His easily recognizable paintings harmoniously combined a classical austerity of design and romantic sensitivity with a subtle taste for a spontaneous perception of nature. The painter was on friendly terms with the Barbizons, but he preferred to work independently because he believed that it was "better to be nothing than to echo some other's painting". His work became a veritable school for the young revolutionaries in painting, the future Impressionists, who dreamed of radical transformations in art.

CLAUDE MONET
(1840–1926)
Poppy Field
Late 1880s

Monet declared: "I would like to be born blind and then suddenly to recover my sight so that I could begin painting without knowing what the objects I am painting are like." These words define the principal idea of his work and the idea of Impressionism as a whole. To work directly from nature and immediately to convey one's impressions recording only the numerous shades of colour ever changing under the action of light — that is the main task faced by Monet and his friends.

CLAUDE MONET (1840–1926)
The Pond at Montgeron
1876

Monet *completely abandoned the traditional understanding of painting and composition evolved in the seventeenth century and exemplified by the classical landscapes of Claude Lorrian. Even the monumental* Pond at Montgeron *painted by the artist for the decoration of the villa of the art collector Hochédé, a financier and an admirer of Impressionism, who were so rare in that period, was executed as an immediate and rapid study out of doors. There are no clear-cut planes in the picture, the objects on the canvas cannot be divided into main and auxiliary ones, and the wide, separate brushstrokes look at a short distance like a chaotic mass of pigments, but at some distance there arises a striking feeling of a real scene vibrant in sunlight, of water glistening with thousands shades and reflecting the masses of trees and the figures of fishermen dissolved by light.*

CAMILLE PISSARRO (1830–1903)
Boulevard Montmartre in Paris
1897

Pissarro was the eldest among the artists who had contacts with the Impressionists, and it was thanks to Monet's influence that he took an interest in the new painterly system devoting much of his works to townscapes. Pissarro focused his work on the image of Paris — he painted the city in spring, in summer, in autumn and in winter, in every time of day, but his Paris invariably looks vivid and festive; it is throbbing with life and filled with movement. His series of Montmartre views consists of thirteen canvases which were painted by the artist from a window of his studio. Captured from above, the city looks as if seen from the bird's-eye-view. It is now crowded with people and carriages, now lit by the warm rays of the sun, now bluish in twilight and now silvery in the rain — it appears different every time.

ALFRED SISLEY (1839–1899)
*Village on the Bank
of the Seine*
1872

Sisley, an Englishman born in Paris, became acquainted with the future Impressionists Monet and Renoir in the 1860s, when he studied in the workshop of the artist and teacher Gleyre. A painter with an unusually refined colouristic gift, Sisley liked to paint the picturesque outskirts of Paris from nature. His works imbued with light seem to be more traditional and quiet than the temperamental and dynamic landscapes by Monet, but Sisley, with his keen feeling of the unpretentious beauty of Île-de-France, attained such a mastery in his landscapes that the most unpretentious study produced by him seemed to be filled with harmony and delicacy.

HENRI FANTIN-LATOUR
(1836–1904)
*Bouquet of Roses and
Nasturtiums in a Vase*
1883

Fantin-Latour was on friendly terms with the Impressionists, but he never joined the group. His work is a specific blend of Realist, Impressionist and Romantic features slightly touched with sweetness characteristic of Salon art. His numerous still lifes depicting bouquets of flowers had a great success with the public. His carefully rendered flower compositions are, however, never mere naturalistic copies from life — they are expressive and poetic visions of nature.

PIERRE AUGUSTE RENOIR
(1841–1919)
*Portrait of the Actress
Jeanne Samary*
1878

It seems that men, women
and children in Renoir's paintings do not pose, but go on
living as usual and have been
just stopped for a moment to be
captured by the swift and light
brush of the talented artist.
Even the charming red-haired
Jeanne Samary, an actress of
the Comédie Française, who is
standing still in front of Renoir
for a classical formal portrait,
seemingly would soon unfold
her arms, smile with her
enchanting smile and swiftly
disappear leaving behind only
a memory of her beautiful blue
eyes, white skin and silk dress
notable for a wealth of its shades.
It is difficult to imagine that
this beautiful woman portrayed
by the delighted Renoir in the
prime of her life, would pass
away at the age of thirty-three.

PIERRE AUGUSTE RENOIR (1841–1919)
Child with a Whip
1885

At first sight Child with a Whip *looks like one of Renoir's masterpieces in the Impressionist style. The artist's main hero in this painting is sunlight. It seems to dissolve the boy's figure in his environment and to colour his white dress and the sandy path with greenish, yellow and bluish tints. However, the oval of the childish face, the dark large eyes and the bright pouting lips of the small boy, whose name was Etienne Goujon, are painted out in a careful and clear-cut manner, apparently different from the Impressionist principles. In the period when this picture was painted, Renoir was searching for a novel artistic manner that would combine the spontaneity of Impressionism and the classical deliberation prevalent in the preceding eighteenth century.*

Cézanne arrived at Paris from his native Aix-en-Provence in the 1860s as a mature and original master. The Impressionists helped him avoid a dark colour scheme, yet his paintings would never adhere to their pictorial system. Cézanne, similarly to the Impressionists, does not dissolve his details in the air medium, yet he neither seeks to render the texture of the objects. The artist models the volumes of the fruit, vessels and the folds of the curtain not by means of light and shade as Old Masters did, but by alternating warm and cold hues. He specially composed his still lifes from simple objects which would resemble a ball, a cylinder or a cone.

PAUL CÉZANNE (1839–1906)
Mont Sainte-Victoire
1900

Cézanne also borrowed from the Impressionists their method of work in the open air. He regarded Pissarro as his teacher because he took his first lessons of plein-air *painting working with Pissarro in the country. But the Impressionists and Cézanne saw nature in a different way. The Mont Sainte-Victoire at Aix, to which Cézanne devoted dozens of his masterpieces, is represented as a majestic and harmonious creation dominating the environment by its rhythms. In the words of one of Cézanne's friends, he "interpreted rather than copied what he saw".

PAUL CÉZANNE (1839–1906)
The Smoker
Ca. 1895

Portraying people, Cézanne did not seek to convey the psychological states or characters of his sitters. Man is for him primarily the most complex and interesting form created by nature. The artist had his models pose for him for a long time, in some cases up to a hundred sittings, trying to understand the austere logic and balance of their structure.

VINCENT VAN GOGH
(1853–1890)
The Lilac Bush
1889

This picture was painted by Van Gogh in the garden of the San-Rémy Hospital where he took cure after one of his usual attacks of mental illness. During a period of temporary abatement of suffering, he created this masterpiece endowing the study with an unusual dramatic feeling and profound symbolic meaning. In the blossoming lilac bush thrusting its branches to the heavens, but firmly rooted in the soil, in the tragic clash of the saturated blue and green shades, Van Gogh expressed his dreams of freedom and harmony in art somewhat darkened by a sense of impossibility to realize these aims.

VINCENT VAN GOGH
(1853–1890)
Cottages
1890

This canvas was painted at Auvers, several months before the artist's tragic death. Van Gogh had no hope to cure from his illness any more. But the painting has no tragic overtones. Evidently the artist himself was satisfied with this work. He wrote to his brother Théo: "I'm painting a study now — old thatched cottages, grain fields and a field of blooming pies in the foreground, with hills in the background. I hope you will like it."

PAUL GAUGUIN (1848–1903)
Pastorales Tahitiennes
1893

Driven by a romantic striving to set himself free from the rigid framework of European art, Gauguin found his "Golden Age" at Tahiti Island. There, amidst naïve aborigines living at one with nature, he created in his pictures a fascinating world of dreams and recollections. His manner of painting is far from a down-to-earth approach, yet real impressions constitute an important element in his work. The canvas is saturated with a musical quality which can be sensed in the rhythm of the twisting trees and flowers and in the soft movements of the Tahitian women. The bright pure colours of the painting suggest a resemblance to mediaeval enamels.

PAUL GAUGUIN (1848–1903)
Sunflowers
1901

This latest of the Hermitage paintings by Gauguin, created at Dominique Island where the artist moved from Tahiti, is filled with mysticism and mystery. Among the large yellow flowers there emerges a widely open eye — the mysterious All-Seeing Eye, and the immobile face is reminiscent of the Buddha's likeness. Christian artists depicted the All-Seeing Eye encircled by rays of sunlight. Did Gauguin associate this picture with Christian symbolism? Its subject matter is merely suggestive of such interpretation, yet it does not give any direct answer.

Signac, together with his friend Georges Seurat, evolved the painterly idiom which became known as Neo-Impressionism or Divisionism, or Pointillism. The artists believed that there was too much casual in Impressionist painting, whereas the method they invented drawing on the scientific principle of the optic mixture of colours divided on the canvas into small strokes would endow the picture with a sense of finish and balance.

PIERRE BONNARD
(1867–1947)
Morning in Paris
1911

Bonnard was a member of the Nabis, a group of artists which emerged in Paris in the 1890s. There is nothing intended for an outward effect in his art, but his keen perception of a true painter capable of capturing the slightest shades of colour; transformed the glimpses of usual Parisian life into perfectly arranged scenes where every detail is important.

MAURICE DENIS (1870–1943)
Spring Landscape with Figures (Sacred Grove)
1897

Denis, *the leader of the Nabis group, relies in his work on the past calling his method Neo-Traditionalism. Infatuated with Gauguin at the start of his career as an artist, he later plunged into a study of Poussin and Italian masters of the Renaissance. The* Sacred Grove *is full of symbols and allusions. The girl in the foreground is writing on a tree stem the artist's signature — evidently Denis hints at the ancient custom according to which a girl was to write the name of her intended bridegroom to make her wish come true. The two naked girls are weaving wreaths of camomiles — a wreath was regarded as a sign of one's destiny, while camomiles were associated with fortune telling in matters of love. A couple of grazing deer in the background are also connected with the symbolism of love. The motifs of spring and love, interwoven in the picture, partly elucidate its mysterious subject matter.*

HENRI MATISSE (1869–1954)
*The Red Room
(Dessert. Harmony in Red)*. 1908

*The main task which Matisse and his friends
the Fauves set for themselves was the liberation
of colour. Matisse often repeated: "I took much
from the Impressionists, but they saw their
colour in nature, whereas I invented it myself."*
The Red Room *could be compared with
a concert for a solo instrument with orchestra,
where the main part is performed by the red
colour. Originally the predominant colour of the
picture was blue and it was called* Harmony
in Blue, *but later, when the work had already
been purchased by Shchukin, Matisse transformed it into* Harmony in Red.

< HENRI MATISSE (1869–1954)
The Dance
1910

Matisse painted two decorative panels, The Dance *and* Music, *for Sergei Shchukin's mansion in Moscow. Matisse told about the concept of this complex: "I am putting myself in the place of a visitor who is coming from outside. I must awaken in him a desire to exert himself, and to do so I must convey a sensation of lightness and ease. My first panel depicts a dance fleeting above a hill…"* The Dance *is not merely a flat colourful panel decorating the interior — Matisse endowed his work with a deep symbolic message.*

HENRI MATISSE (1869–1954)
Conversation
1909

This *large-scale composition with a predominant pure blue is a complex combination of a decorative panel and a portrait. It shows Matisse himself and his wife Amélie. Although the artist denied that he had set for himself the task of painting a portrait, nevertheless there is a kind of dialogue based on the juxtaposition of the two strong personalities, the two conventional but strikingly lifelike figures standing out against the blue plane of the background. The blue here is the colour of the shadow in which the room is steeped, while the pink rectangular of the window, through which a blossoming garden can be seen, evokes a sensation of sunlit space.*

O*ne of Picasso's best works from the Blue Period, this lofty and somewhat generalized composition, full of drama, was created by the artist on the basis of real impressions and numerous sketches from life. The young Picasso, soon after his twenty-first birthday, preferred to find characters for his work during that period of his life in Paris among miserable and poor people. At the gate of the Saint-Lazare Hospital he saw two sisters one of which was a nun and the other a harlot. But real characters have lost their concrete features in the painting. Picasso's heroines are symbols of solitude and suffering in the alien world filled with a cold blue colour. A feeling of tragic hopelessness dominating the canvas and the artist's preference for a blue tonality used to convey his main concept, reveal some resemblance of this painting by the great master to works by Luis de Morales, Picasso's fellow-countryman who had lived more than three centuries before.*

PABLO PICASSO (1881–1973)
Woman with a Fan (After a Ball)
1908

I*n 1906 Picasso arrived at the new painterly system which later took shape under the name of Cubism. The artist began to create his own world, not connected with real impressions but consisting of geometrical structures and volumes. The great Cézanne once said that everything in nature could be reduced to a ball, cylinder and cone. Picasso followed the behest of his idol developing his idea to the logical end. Other source of his inspiration was Negro sculpture with its free treatment of real forms. The artist seems to construct his characters of crudely hewn geometrical figures without, however, depriving them of human emotions. The posture of his Cubist* Woman with a Fan *is absolutely natural — she is seated in an armchair in an easy, relaxed manner; her head is drooping and her hand seems to hold the fan with difficulty.*

PABLO PICASSO (1881–1973)
The Dance of the Veils
1907

The painting is imbued with dynamism, which is unusual for Picasso's static Cubist paintings. The woman's figure made up of simple geometrical shapes seems to be pervaded with a turbulent rhythm of a passionate Spanish dance. A sense of whirlwind movement is emphasized by the diagonals of the shroud streaming up, the movement of the arms and legs agreeing with the furious sounds of music. The incised lines covering the body of the Cubist dancer create an illusion of a slender rounded figure with a thin waist and high breast; the face looks like a stiff mask stressing the deep concentration of the dancer.

Russian
Painting
13th to 20th Century

The Hermitage's collection of Russian painting is very specific in character. It is part of the Department of the History of Russian Culture, the youngest in the museum, organized in the 1940s.

Catherine the Great created the Hermitage as a museum of foreign art. Of course she did commission works from Russian artists, chiefly the portraits that decorated her palaces, but they were not regarded as museum exhibits. Icons, even ancient examples, were looked on exclusively as religious objects. The major successes achieved by Russia in the fine arts by the nineteenth century prompted Alexander I to create a department of Russian painting in the Hermitage and in 1802 the active acquisition of paintings by contemporary artists began. When, in the middle of the century, a special building was constructed for the museum alongside the Winter Palace, two of its large halls were given over to the paintings of major Russian artists. In 1898, however, these were all transferred to the newly-opened Russian Museum in St Petersburg, that was specially dedicated to the country's own art. This museum and the slightly older Tretyakov Gallery in Moscow present an exhaustive picture of the evolution of Russian art over many centuries. The Russian Department of the Hermitage was created with different goals: its exhibits, among which historical and cultural valuables, objects of applied art, and items of everyday use predominate, reflect some of the most important events in the history of the Russian State and the many sides of its rich culture and art.

The material transferred to the museum from various sources in the 1940s for the new department included a group of icons. In the years that followed it expanded many times over with works purchased from or donated by private individuals, and also the products of the museum's regular scholarly expeditions. Under Soviet power the majority of places of worship in Russia were closed. Many icons that had belonged to them were kept in totally unsuitable conditions and were doomed to perish. It was with the aim of studying works of ecclesiastical architecture and saving valuable examples of Early Russian art that from the early 1950s the Hermitage's researchers and restorers began travelling to different parts of Russia, above all the remote European north. Every expedition brought interesting finds, but the icons were as a rule in poor condition and needed urgent restoration. The Hermitage's specialists devoted many years to saving these works, strengthening the old panels on which the icons were painted, removing blackened oil varnish and later overpainting, to reveal the original images.

Today the Hermitage possesses a valuable collection of Russian icons dating from the late thirteenth to the early twentieth centuries. It includes both large church icons and family ones that are sometimes miniature in size. They are connected to various schools and reflect all the main tendencies in Russian ecclesiastical art.

The earliest belong to the Novgorod school. Novgorod the Great was one of the oldest and most important centres of Early Russian art. Located in north-western Russia, this large trading city avoided the attacks of the Tatar-Mongols and its development proceeded uninterrupted for many centuries. In rethinking the traditional Byzantine images, Novgorod artists included in them a good deal from folk art. Their works are marked by bright, joyful colours, in which red and golden ochre are dominant. The compositions of the icons are forcefully simple as a rule, but in some cases they contain a detailed account of an event, include allegorical figures and symbolic detail of various kinds. This is true of the large Novgorod icon of *The Last Judgement* from the first half of the sixteenth century, one of the best in the museum. Its creator was a splendid artist, but, like the majority of Early Russian painters, he remained anonymous. The icon-painters looked on their work as an act of religious devotion and did not sign their pieces. Old chronicles and documents have preserved only a few names of the greatest artists of Early Russia.

Somewhat later than in Novgorod a distinctive school of icon-painting formed in Pskov, the second important centre of north-western Russia. Pskov painting is a little archaic, austere and solemn. In contrast to the bright colours typical of Novgorod icons, its colour scheme is more reserved. Often murky, disturbing tones give Pskov icons a sense of drama and tension. This school is particularly interesting for innovations in iconography.

Besides the Novgorod and Pskov, there were many other local schools, each with its own character and traditions. In the later fourteenth century the Moscow school began to flourish. It is associated with the work of one of the greatest Early Russian artists, Andrei Rublev. Few of that master's works have survived and there are none in the Hermitage, but a number of the icons reflect the new features that he contributed to Russian icon-painting: moral purity, humanity and profound emotional undertones in the images.

A special place in the Hermitage collection is taken by a group of icons, unrivalled in size, connected with the Russian North, examples of "Northern Painting". These icons were created by artists from different places. Some worked in the large workshops attached to monasteries; others were lone craftsmen, but their works have certain similar features that set them apart from the icons produced in other artistic centres of Russia. The northern artists treated traditional subjects and images in a free manner. They had their own favourite saints, among whom Nicholas and George were especially venerated.

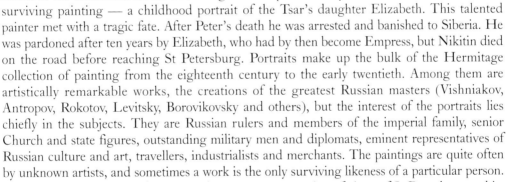

Despite the canonical requirements on church art, Russian icon-painting did change with time. Each era contributed something new to it. In the late icons there is a noticeable influence of secular painting that appeared in Russia in the seventeenth century and began to develop rapidly in the eighteenth, under the Tsar-Reformer Peter the Great.

The profound changes in all aspects of life that took place in Peter's time, and particularly a new attitude to the individual were reflected in portraiture. This genre dominated in Russian art throughout the eighteenth century. The first major Russian painter of the new era was a portraitist, Ivan Nikitin, whom Peter sent to study in Italy and appointed court painter on his return to his homeland. In the Hermitage he is represented by his earliest surviving painting — a childhood portrait of the Tsar's daughter Elizabeth. This talented painter met with a tragic fate. After Peter's death he was arrested and banished to Siberia. He was pardoned after ten years by Elizabeth, who had by then become Empress, but Nikitin died on the road before reaching St Petersburg. Portraits make up the bulk of the Hermitage collection of painting from the eighteenth century to the early twentieth. Among them are artistically remarkable works, the creations of the greatest Russian masters (Vishniakov, Antropov, Rokotov, Levitsky, Borovikovsky and others), but the interest of the portraits lies chiefly in the subjects. They are Russian rulers and members of the imperial family, senior Church and state figures, outstanding military men and diplomats, eminent representatives of Russian culture and art, travellers, industrialists and merchants. The paintings are quite often by unknown artists, and sometimes a work is the only surviving likeness of a particular person.

One further group of paintings, less numerous, consists of views of St Petersburg and its environs, showing how the capital of Russia looked at various times, and also interior views of the Winter Palace and other architectural landmarks of the city. These paintings are again important above all as historical records

A very valuable addition to the painting collection of the Russian Department are the works of the great artist of the first half of the twentieth century Wassily Kandinsky. A Russian by birth, Kandinsky got his professional training in Munich although, by his own admission, he was first inspired to take up painting seriously by his acquaintance with Russian folk art and icons. Works of that kind to a large extent influenced his perception of colour. The first phase of Kandinsky's career took place in Germany. In 1914, when war broke out, he returned to Moscow where he worked intensively until the early 1920s. In 1921 when the artist left Russia, his Moscow studio contained a large number of paintings that ended up in the Museum of New Western Art, created from the works formerly owned by the major collectors Shchukin, Morozov, Riabushinsky and others. In 1948 the Soviet leadership decided to do away with the Museum of New Western Art. Orders were given to distribute the exhibits to provincial museums (with the exception of some that were to be destroyed). The Hermitage managed to obtain some of the best Kandinskys, but they were kept for a long time in the closed stocks and only put on display in the early 1970s.

Icon:
The Intercession
15th century
The Pskov school

The icon comes from the Church of the Intercession in Pskov. In the central part of the church the Virgin can be seen on a cloud in a praying attitude. Above Her are the figure of the blessing Christ and Angels who are holding the shroud. In the aisles are the figures of saints. The composition, traditional for Russian icons, expresses the idea of the Virgin's patronage to believers.

Icon:
St Nicholas
Late 15th or early 16th century
The Northern school

St Nicholas is one of the most popular saints of the Orthodox Church. His worship was widespread on the vast territory of the Russian North. He was depicted as an old man wearing bishop's garments. The miracle worker and patron of the people, St Nicholas is holding the Gospels in his left hand and his right hand is blessing people. The terse composition of the icon with the majestic figure against a light background is reminiscent of frescoes on church walls.

Icon:
The Miracle of St George
Late 15th or early 16th century
The Northern school

The subject of this icon coming from Archangel Region and executed by a local Northern artist is based on a story about one of miraculous deeds of St George. He is shown as a young warrior mounted on a white horse and striking the Dragon with his spear. In comparison with Novgorod icons where this motif had been treated for the first time, this icon looks more archaic yet expressive in its own way. The diagonals enhance the expressiveness of the composition. St George the Warrior was one of the most popular saints in Russia as a personification of the victory of the good over the evil.

Icon:
The Last Judgement
First half of the 16th century
The Novgorod school

The elaborate composition of this colourful Novgorod icon serves to represent a symbolic picture of the world — the heavens shaped as a scroll with the sun, moon and stars; Christ the Judge encircled by the Angels and Saints; people going to the judgement and the Angels and Devils fighting for their souls in the middle tier; below them Paradise and Hell are shown.

IVAN VISHNIAKOV (1699–1761)
Portrait of Stepanida Yakovleva
1756

The works of Ivan Vishniakov, a major artist of the mid-eighteenth century, are notable for a distinctly national feature — a wealth of ornamentation which suggests his love for the traditions of Russian folk art. His portrait of a young well-dressed girl from a merchant family, with a rosy face and jet-black hair, who seems to be arrested in a majestic posture, was executed by the artist on the occasion of her marriage to the son of the well-known St Petersburg businessman Savva Yakovlev.

IVAN NIKITIN (CA. 1680–1742)
Portrait of Elizabeth Petrovna as a Child
Ca. 1712

Peter the Great called Ivan Nikitin, the first important portrait painter in the history of Russian art, "a kind master". He had produced this portrait of the Tsar's daughter even before he was sent to Italy for training. The portrait showing Elizabeth at the age of three, reveals the artist's great natural gifts and his ability to penetrate into the inner world of his sitters. According to the etiquette, Elizabeth wears a formal dress and her hair is elaborately dressed in an adult manner. However, the tilt of her head and a pensive look lend to the image of the girl an unofficial, deeply intimate character.

WASSILY KANDINSKY
(1866–1944)
Composition No. 6
1913

Kandinsky created his first
abstract works, the earliest
in European painting, as early
as the late 1900s. He divided
them into purely intuitive
"improvisations", "impressions" inspired by some natural
motifs and monumental "compositions" to which he attached
a special importance. Composition No 6 ranks with
the best works of the latter
type. Kandinsky compared
the art of the painter working
in colours and lines with the
art of the composer creating
by means of sounds.

Plan of the museum
exhibitions

1st FLOOR
PALACE SQUARE

MILLIONNAYA STREET

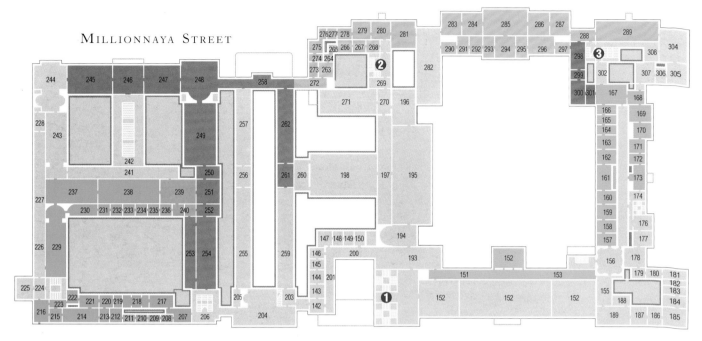

PALACE EMBANKMENT

2nd FLOOR
PALACE SQUARE

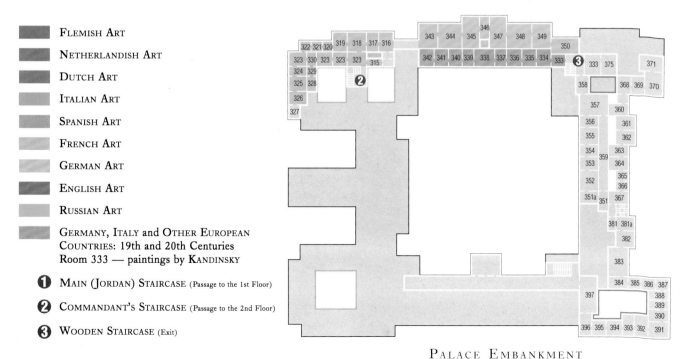

PALACE EMBANKMENT

FLEMISH ART

NETHERLANDISH ART

DUTCH ART

ITALIAN ART

SPANISH ART

FRENCH ART

GERMAN ART

ENGLISH ART

RUSSIAN ART

GERMANY, ITALY AND OTHER EUROPEAN
COUNTRIES: 19th and 20th Centuries
Room 333 — paintings by KANDINSKY

❶ MAIN (JORDAN) STAIRCASE (Passage to the 1st Floor)

❷ COMMANDANT'S STAIRCASE (Passage to the 2nd Floor)

❸ WOODEN STAIRCASE (Exit)